PLANT-BASED DIET FOR BEGINNERS

Optimal Health, Weight, & Well—Being with Delicious, Affordable, & Easy Recipes, Habits, and Lifestyle Hacks

MADISON FULLER

FREE BONUS

https://www.subscribepage.com/hba_copy

PLANT-BASED DIET FOR BEGINNERS

INTRODUCTION
THE POWER OF A PLANT-BASED DIET

Have you ever tried going on a plant-based diet?

For a lot of people, going plant-based means only eating soy products, salads, and other boring dishes. But this couldn't be further from the truth. A plant-based diet is rich in nutrients, content, and taste. Simply put, plant-based diets are diets that focus on foods taken from plant sources such as vegetables, fruits, nuts, seeds, legumes, and more.

The great thing about going plant-based is that you can create your own personalized plan based on your preferences. You can go completely plant-based without eating any animal-based foods or you can continue eating small amounts of animal products such as eggs and dairy while focusing mainly on plant sources. You don't have to be too strict with yourself. Instead, you can diversify your diet by discovering how truly delicious plant-based foods can be.

These days, prioritizing your health is of the essence. You want to be at the peak of your health in order to avoid illnesses. One of the best ways to do this is by improving your diet. You can do this by adding more plants to your plate.

This book will help you out.

It's the perfect book for beginner to intermediate cooks who want to eat healthier foods. This book includes recipes for breakfast, lunch, dinner, snacks, smoothies, soups, and more. If you're looking for easy, delicious, simple, and inexpensive recipes to make, this is the cookbook for you!

To make things easy for you, the recipes here are neatly organized. They also use ingredients that you either have at home or are easy to get at the store. Each recipe includes the ingredients, steps, and even basic nutritional information. The latter can be very helpful if you want to achieve weight loss and other health goals.

Going plant-based doesn't always mean becoming healthier. For instance, if you only focus on packaged or processed foods, you might end up compromising your health instead of improving it. To gain all the benefits of this type of diet, it's better to use fresh ingredients to create nutrient-dense dishes that will fill you up and make you feel satisfied.

As someone who has successfully transitioned to a plant-based diet, I can tell you that it comes with many wonderful benefits. Since going plant-based, I have lost some weight, have higher energy levels, and I also feel amazing! I also discovered how truly diverse plant sources are. By combining different ingredients, you can create amazingly delectable and nutritious dishes that will keep you wanting more.

For several years, I have tried making different types of plant-based dishes. I even tried recipes from different cuisines. The great thing about these recipes is that many of them are totally customizable, which means that you can mix and match the ingredients according to your preferences. After trying countless recipes, I gathered some of the best, most flavorful dishes to create this cookbook. By the end of this book, you will have tons of recipes to try at home— recipes that will bring you closer to your health goals.

Is your mouth watering yet?

Keep turning the pages to learn more!

CHAPTER 1
WHAT IS A PLANT-BASED DIET?

These days, there are so many diets to choose from. All of these diets have their own rules and health claims. But if you try to examine most of the trendiest diets, you will discover that most of them emphasize the consumption of fresh, whole, and natural foods while minimizing your intake of processed or packaged foods. Doing this improves your overall health as you would nourish your body with the proper foods.

By going plant-based, you can gain the benefits of the healthiest diets simply because plant-based diets focus on the consumption of whole, healthy foods. For such diets, you would focus on plant sources. The type of plant-based diet you would follow depends on you. The different types are:

- A flexitarian or semi-vegetarian diet

where you would eat dairy products and eggs. On this diet, you would also eat seafood, poultry, fish, and meat occasionally.

- A pescatarian diet where you would eat seafood, fish, eggs, and dairy products. However, you wouldn't eat any poultry or meat.

- A vegan diet where you would only eat plant foods and avoid animal foods completely.

- A vegetarian or lacto-ovo vegetarian diet where you would only eat dairy products and eggs, but no seafood, poultry, fish, or meat.

The great thing about going plant-based is that you have the freedom to decide what to include in your meals. You don't have to stick to a schedule and you don't have to follow strict rules either. This allows you to enjoy your transition while eventually gaining all the benefits that plant-based diets have to offer.

The Benefits of a Plant-Based Diet

Going plant-based is a significant step you can take to improve your overall health. By focusing on whole, fresh, plant-based foods, you can gain many benefits over time. Let's take a look at these potential benefits to inspire you to start changing your diet for the better.

Promotes Weight Loss

One of the most significant benefits of plant-based diets is that they can help you lose weight. Most plant foods are high in fiber, which means that they are more filling. By cooking your own plant-based meals at home, you can enjoy dishes that will make you feel satisfied and full for longer periods of time. This, in turn, reduces your overall caloric intake, which then leads to weight loss.

Supports the Immune System

Plant foods contain essential nutrients that aren't available in animal foods. These include some types of vitamins, minerals, antioxidants, and phytochemicals that promote the health of your cells while maintaining the balance of hormones in your body. All of these effects support your immune system, which is essential for your overall health.

Reduces Inflammation

Inflammation is a normal bodily function. It occurs when foreign objects, bacteria, irritants, and other threats go into your body and your white blood cells fight these invaders off. Once the threat is gone, the inflammation should go away too. However, prolonged or chronic inflammation isn't good as it can damage your body's tissues and cells.

Fortunately, the essential nutrient content of plant foods helps reduce inflammation in the body. Specifically, the antioxidants and phytochemicals that promote the health of your immune system also help neutralize the toxins in your body to reduce and even prevent inflammation. They also combat free radicals that cause damage to your cells.

Promotes Gut Health

Plant-based diets can also keep your gut healthy thanks to the nutrient content of plant foods. The fiber content of plant foods also contributes to this benefit. This is a significant benefit since a healthy gut promotes proper metabolism, healthy bowel movements, strong immunity, and good hormonal balance. With a strong and healthy gut, your body is able to absorb the nutrients from the food you eat more efficiently. This creates a beneficial cycle that will keep you at the peak of your health.

Protects You From Disease

With all the benefits mentioned above, your body will also be strong enough to protect itself from disease. This is especially true for chronic diseases like diabetes, heart disease, kidney problems, arthritis, cognitive decline, and even cancer. By focusing more on whole, healthy plant foods, you can protect yourself by lowering your risk for these diseases. This, in turn, can even help you live longer!

These are just some of the most significant benefits of plant-based diets. There are many more. Since following such a diet can be as simple as adding more greens to your plate, you can see why more and more people have decided to follow this trend.

Beginner Tips for You

Now that you have a better understanding of plant-based diets and their benefits to health, you should feel motivated to start your plant-based journey right away! As mentioned, doing this is easy since you have the freedom to choose what type of plant-based diet to follow. Whichever you choose, these tips can help you out:

- Try to change your mindset in terms of the food you eat. For instance, if you have always thought that veggies are only meant as a side dish, start thinking of them as the main course with meat, seafood, poultry, or fish as side dishes to your meals.

- Start gradually. Cook one plant-based meal for yourself once or twice a week. After one or two weeks, increase this to two or three plant-based meals a week. Keep going until you reach your goal

- Make it a habit to fill your plate with vegetables at every meal, even for snacks or dessert! Add veggies of all colors to your plate and enjoy "eating the rainbow."

- Learn how to build your meals around simple plant dishes. For instance, you can start with a salad, then add different ingredients to add flavors and textures to it.

- Get used to eating healthy plant-based fat sources like olive oil, seeds, nuts, nut butters, and avocados, for instance. These will make your meals more satisfying.

- Learn how to cook plant-based foods in different ways. Experiment with cooking techniques like stir-frying, braising, steaming, grilling, and more. These preserve the nutritional content while bringing out the flavors of each ingredient in the dish.

- Find ways to transform your favorite dishes to make them plant-based. You can do this by switching any animal-based ingredients to plant-based ones. For instance, you can use agave or maple syrup instead of honey, tofu instead of chicken or seafood, and more.

- Diversify your diet by discovering how to make dishes from different cuisines. These days, it's very easy to find vegan and vegetarian recipes from all over the world. You can even find some of these recipes in this cookbook! By trying out different ingredients and cuisines, you will make your diet more interesting.

Finally, prepare and cook your own meals at home! There is nothing more satisfying and comforting than a meal you prepared for yourself. Since this is a cookbook, you already have the perfect tool to do this. Then all you have to do is to follow the recipes to discover how tasty and satisfying plant-based dishes can be!

CHAPTER 2
MEAL PLANNING ON A PLANT-BASED DIET?

One great way to start a new diet and make sure that you stick with it is by meal planning. This is a simple process that involves planning your meals for a certain amount of time, then set a schedule to cook those meals. For instance, you can plan your menu for a week on Monday morning, then buy all of the ingredients you need in the afternoon. On Tuesday morning, you would prep all of the ingredients and cook all of the meals you have planned the previous day.

After cooking all of the dishes and allowing them to cool down completely, you would store them in containers, add labels, and store all of them in the refrigerator. This gives you a whole week of delicious, homemade meals to look forward to for the rest of the week. All you have to do is to heat up the dishes and enjoy!

Meal planning has gained a lot of popularity in recent years. It's ideal for people who want to eat healthier, save money, save time, and enjoy meals that they have cooked themselves. Although meal planning does take some getting used to, when you get the hang of the process, you will discover why it's so practical and efficient. Get started with meal planning by following these tips:

- Before creating your menu, check your stocks in the kitchen. Find out what ingredients you already have so you can use those in the dishes you will cook. This will help you save money while reducing food waste. Also, check for any leftovers in the refrigerator from the previous week so you can include them in your menu.

- Try to find the balance between dishes that use the same ingredients yet have different flavor profiles. That way, you won't get bored with the meals you eat each day.

- If you're still in the process of transitioning into a plant-based diet, include a combination of animal-based dishes, plant-based dishes, and even dishes that combine both ingredients.

- Find ways to use the same ingredients in different ways. This is especially important for ingredients like grains, greens, and even seasonal veggies. Such ingredients will make your dishes healthier, more filling, and more interesting too.

- Try to avoid complex dishes or recipes that include ingredients that are too exotic. Save these dishes for special occasions or days when you have a lot of time to learn new cooking techniques and recipes that have plenty of complicated steps. Remember, meal planning is all about convenience and efficiency.

- If you're cooking for your family too, ask for their input when creating your menu. Try to encourage them to eat plant-based dishes too by letting them try the amazing dishes you will learn in this cookbook. That way, you won't have to cook different meals at home as this takes more time and effort.

It's also a good idea to invest in high-quality kitchen tools and appliances a little bit at a time. Having these things will make you feel more motivated to keep cooking delicious dishes while establishing healthier eating habits in the process.

Foods to Eat

Following a plant-based diet isn't about restricting yourself or counting calories. It's more about making small yet significant changes to your diet in favor of plant-based foods. Plant-based diets are wonderful because when it comes to food choices, there are countless options! To give you a better idea of how diverse your diet can be, let's take a look at the foods you can eat on a plant-based diet.

PLANT-BASED DIET FOR BEGINNERS

- Condiments like mustard, nutritional yeast, salsa, soy sauce, vinegar, and more.

- Fruits like apples, bananas, berries, citrus fruits, grapes, oranges, peaches, pears, and more.

- Healthy fats like avocados, coconut, olive oil, and more.

- Herbs, spices, and seasonings like basil, garlic, ginger, pepper, salt, turmeric, and more.

- Nuts and seeds like almonds, cashews, chia seeds, flax seeds, walnuts, and more.

- Nut butter like almond butter, cashew butter, peanut butter, and more.

- Plant-based cheese, cream, and yogurt.

- Plant-based protein sources like plant-based protein powders, tempeh, tofu, and more.

- Plant milk like almond milk, cashew milk, and more.

- Pulses like beans and legumes.

- Root vegetables like carrots, parsnips,

17

potatoes, sweet potatoes, and more.

- Vegetables like asparagus, collard greens, corn, cruciferous veggies, eggplants, leafy greens, peas, peppers, and more.

- Whole grains like barley, brown rice, cereals, oats, popcorn, quinoa, whole wheat, and more.

When planning your meals, it's a good idea to check the nutrient content of the foods you eat. Do this to make sure that you are nourishing your body with all of the vitamins and minerals it needs every day.

Foods to Avoid

While you don't have to eliminate all animal-based foods from your diet right away, you should know which foods to avoid or limit if you really want to transition into a plant-based diet. Let's take a look at these foods.

- Bacon, hotdogs, sausages, and other processed meat products.

- Beef, mutton, pork, veal, and other types of meat.

- Butter, honey, margarine, and other oils derived from animals.

- Cheese, milk, yogurt, and other types of dairy products.

- Chicken, duck, turkey, and other types of poultry including eggs.

- Clams, crabs, mussels, shrimp, and other types of seafood.

- Mackerel, salmon, sardines, tuna, and other types of fish.

If animal products are currently part of your diet, you don't have to stop eating them right away. For your transition to go smoothly, it's best to gradually phase these foods out of your diet.

Fortunately, it's quite easy to differentiate plant-based foods from animal-based foods. But you should know that animal products can also be used as ingredients in various food items. This is where the challenge lies. To make sure that your diet remains plant-based, make it a habit to read food labels. Or you can just avoid processed food items altogether since they aren't good for you anyway.

Stocking up Your Kitchen

If you want to make it easier to stick with meal planning and your plant-based diet, the best thing you can do is to keep your pantry well-stocked. Having a well-stocked kitchen or pantry is an excellent way to make your meal prep process easier. When you have enough stocks, it will be much easier for you to create a menu every week.

It would also be easier for you to cook various snacks, desserts, and meals whenever you feel like it because you would have all of the ingredients you need on hand. When it comes to keeping food stocks, focus on non-perishable food items like the following:

- Baking essentials like different types of

flour, baking powder, cornstarch, baking soda, and so on.

- Condiments and sauces like tahini, soy sauce, mustard, tamari, and so on.

- Dried or canned beans and legumes.

- Fruits like bananas, pears, apples, melons, grapes, and so on.

- Herbs and spices like rosemary, dill, basil, parsley, cinnamon, ginger, turmeric, salt, pepper, seasoning blends, and so on.

- Jarred or canned vegetables like peppers, corn, peas, tomatoes, olives, and so on.

- Nuts and seeds like walnuts, macadamia nuts, cashews, sunflower seeds, chia seeds, and so on.

- Plant-based milk and nut butter.

- Plant-based oils like avocado oil, peanut oil, vegetable oil, olive oil, coconut oil, and so on.

- Whole grains like brown rice, quinoa, whole-wheat flour, oats, and so on.

Having these foods on hand will make you feel more confident about following your new diet. After planning your menu, make a list of all the other ingredients you need. You can also buy perishable food items like vegetables and some types of fruits regularly. Just make sure to consume them immediately or use them in your dishes right away so they don't get spoiled. Now that you know what food items to stock up in your pantry, it's time to learn how to make the most of your plant-based diet by cooking your own meals at home.

CHAPTER 3
TASTY AND HEALTHY
BREAKFAST RECIPES

Breakfast is the most important meal of the day. It fills you up and nourishes you. It also gives you the energy to complete all of your tasks in the morning without feeling tired. To make sure that you get all the energy you need, it's important to whip up healthy and filling dishes for breakfast. You will learn some amazing choices in this chapter.

Berry French Toast

Even without eggs, you can enjoy French toast, a classic breakfast dish. Here, you will be using aquafaba, a common ingredient in plant-based cooking.

Time	40 minutes
Serving Size	2 servings
Prep Time	10 minutes
Cook Time	30 minutes

Nutritional Facts:
Calories: 429 kcal
Carbs: 49.4 grams
Fat: 25.3 grams
Protein: 9.2 grams

Ingredients for the French toast:

- ⅛ tsp cinnamon (ground)
- ¼ tbsp orange zest (freshly grated)
- 1 tbsp pure maple syrup
- ¼ cup of almond flour
- ½ cup of aquafaba
- ¾ cup almond milk (unsweetened, unflavored)
- A pinch of salt
- 4 slices of bread (preferably whole-grain)

Ingredients for the berry compote:

- ½ tsp pure maple syrup
- ¼ cup of applesauce (homemade or store-bought)
- ½ cup of blueberries (fresh, you can also use raspberries)

Directions:

1. To make the aquafaba, you will need the liquid in a can of chickpeas. Pour the liquid into a bowl.
2. Use a hand mixer to whip the liquid for about 3 to 6 minutes until semi-firm peaks form. Set aside.
3. Preheat your oven to 400˚F. Prepare a baking sheet by placing a wire rack over it.

4. In a bowl, add the aquafaba, cinnamon, salt, almond milk, almond flour, and 1 tablespoon of maple syrup. Mix well until smooth.

5. Pour the mixture into a shallow pan. Add the orange zest, then mix until well combined.

6. Heat a skillet over medium-low heat.

7. Once the skillet is hot enough, place one bread slice into the shallow pan.

8. Soak both sides of the bread slice with the mixture, then place it in the skillet. Cook each side for about 2 to 3 minutes.

9. Place the bread slice on the wire rack on the baking sheet.

10. Repeat the cooking steps for the remaining bread slices.

11. After cooking all of the bread slices, place the baking sheet in the oven. Bake the French toast for about 10 to 15 minutes.

12. While the French toast is baking, prepare the berry compote. In a blender, add all of the compote ingredients.

13. Blend until you get a smooth or chunky consistency, whichever you desire.

14. Take the baking sheet out of the oven and prepare two plates. Place two pieces of French toast on each plate.

15. Drizzle the berry compote over the

French toast.
16. Serve while warm.

Egyptian—Style Breakfast Bowl

This dish is a traditional breakfast option in Egypt and it's usually made using dried fava beans. You can use canned fava beans but if you want to create an authentic dish, using dried beans is the way to go.

Time	1 hour, 40 minutes
Serving Size	2 servings
Prep Time	10 minutes
Cook Time	1 hour, 30 minutes

Nutritional Facts:
Calories: 600 kcal
Carbs: 103.2 grams
Fat: 2.9 grams
Protein: 45.1 grams

Ingredients:

- ½ tsp cumin (ground)
- 1 ½ cups of fava beans (dried, soaked in a bowl of water for 10 hours)
- 1 small yellow onion (peeled, finely diced)
- 2 cloves of garlic (peeled, minced)
- ½ lemon (zest and juice)
- Sea salt
- Water (for cooking the fava beans)
- ½ lemon (sliced into wedges, for serving)

Directions:

1. In a pot, add the fava beans and enough water to cover them completely. Place over high heat, then bring to a boil.
2. Once boiling, turn the head down to medium. Cover the pot and cook the fava beans for about 1 ½ hour until tender.
3. When the fava beans are almost done, prepare the other ingredients. Heat a skillet over medium heat.
4. Once the skillet is hot enough, add the onion. Cook for about 8 to 10 minutes.
5. Add the lemon juice, lemon zest, cumin, and garlic. Cook for about 5 minutes while stirring frequently.
6. Take ½ cup of the cooking liquid from

the pot of fava beans and add it to the skillet.

7. Season with salt and mix well.
8. Drain the rest of the liquid from the pot, then add the fava beans to the skillet. Mix well.
9. Divide the mixture into two bowls.
10. Garnish each bowl with lemon wedges and serve while hot.

Classic Pancakes

Pancakes are another classic breakfast dish. When you follow a plant-based diet, you can still enjoy a hot stack of pancakes by making them using the right ingredients.

Time	20 minutes
Serving Size	2 servings
Prep Time	10 minutes
Cook Time	10 minutes

Nutritional Facts:
Calories: 129 kcal
Carbs: 16.4 grams
Fat: 5.8 grams
Protein: 4 grams

Ingredients:

- ⅛ tsp cinnamon (ground)
- ¼ tsp salt
- ½ tbsp baking powder
- 1 tbsp light brown sugar (you can also use granulated sugar)
- 1 tbsp oil
- 1 tbsp peanut butter (creamy, you can also use cashew butter or almond butter)
- ¼ cup of all-purpose flour
- ¼ cup of whole-wheat flour
- ¾ cup of almond milk (you can also use oat milk)
- Cooking spray
- Maple syrup (for serving)

Directions:

1. In a bowl, add the whole-wheat flour, almond flour, baking powder, cinnamon, salt, and sugar. Mix well.
2. In a cup, add the peanut butter and oil. Whisk well.
3. Add the mixture to the bowl along with the almond milk. Mix well until smooth.
4. Use cooking spray to grease a skillet over low heat.
5. Once the oil is hot enough, pour ¼ cup of batter into it. Swirl the skillet around to

form a pancake shape.

6. Cook the pancake for about 4 to 5 minutes until you see bubbles on the surface.

7. Flip the pancake over and cook for about 3 to 4 minutes.

8. Place the cooked pancake on a plate.

9. Repeat the cooking steps for the remaining pancakes.

10. Serve while hot with maple syrup and fresh fruits if desired.

Veggie Breakfast Burrito

This dish is filled with plant-based protein making it one nutritious breakfast option. It also includes vegan cheese to make it extra tasty.

Time	55 minutes (pressing time not included)
Serving Size	4 servings
Prep Time	15 minutes
Cook Time	40 minutes

Nutritional Facts:
Calories: 472 kcal
Carbs: 58 grams
Fat: 18 grams
Protein: 25 grams

Ingredients for the tofu crumbles:

- ¼ tsp sea salt
- 1 tsp smoked paprika
- 1 tbsp cumin (ground)
- 1 tbsp olive oil
- ¼ cup of soy sauce (preferably low-sodium)
- 1 block of tofu (extra firm)

Ingredients for the burritos:

- 1 tbsp olive oil
- ½ cup of salsa (homemade or store-bought)
- 1 cup of refried beans (canned)
- ½ onion (sliced)
- 1 block of vegan cheddar cheese (shredded)
- 2 bell peppers (seeds removed, sliced)
- 4 tortillas
- Salt
- Cooking spray

Directions:

1. Wrap the block of tofu in a clean cheesecloth, then place something heavy on top of it.
2. Press the tofu for about 15 minutes.

3. Preheat your oven to 400 °F. Use cooking spray to lightly grease two baking sheets.

4. In a bowl, add the soy sauce, olive oil, cumin, paprika, and salt.

5. Remove the heavy object on top of the block of tofu, then remove the cheesecloth.

6. Crumble the pressed tofu, then add the crumbled bits into the bowl with the marinade.

7. Pour the mixture into one of the baking sheets and arrange it in one layer.

8. Place the baking sheet in the oven. Bake the tofu crumbles for about 40 minutes. After 20 minutes, take the baking sheet out, then stir the tofu crumbles around.

9. On the second baking sheet, add the onions, peppers, olive oil, and salt. Toss to coat the vegetables, then arrange them in one layer.

10. Take the baking sheet with the tofu crumbles out of the oven and place the baking sheet with the veggies in the oven.

11. Roast the veggies for about 35 minutes. Halfway through the cooking time, take the baking sheet out and stir the veggies around.

12. After roasting, take the second baking sheet out of the oven.

13. Place one tortilla on a plate. Spoon some refried beans in the middle of the tortilla, then spread it around.
14. Top with roasted veggies, tofu crumbles, salsa, and vegan cheese.
15. Roll the tortilla up tightly to make a burrito.
16. Repeat the assembling steps to make the remaining burritos.
17. Serve immediately or warm the burritos up in the oven before serving.

Coconut Pudding

This breakfast bowl is smooth and tasty. It's an incredible combination of a smoothie bowl and porridge. And it contains just the right combination of ingredients to make you feel full and satisfied.

Time	5 minutes
Serving Size	1 serving
Prep Time	5 minutes
Cook Time	no cooking time

Nutritional Facts:
Calories: 474 kcal
Carbs: 89.8 grams
Fat: 9.2 grams
Protein: 13.4 grams

Ingredients:

- ¼ tsp cinnamon
- ¼ tsp maca powder
- ⅓ cup of coconut flour
- ½ cup of oat milk (hot)
- ½ cup of water (hot)
- 1 banana (puréed)
- A pinch of vanilla (ground)
- Toppings like cocoa nibs, berries, or buckwheat groats

Directions:

1. In a bowl, combine the hot water, hot oat milk, and coconut flour. Mix well.
2. In a blender, add the vanilla, maca, cinnamon, and banana purée. Blend until creamy.
3. Pour the mixture into the bowl with the water, milk, and flour. Mix well.
4. Top with preferred toppings, then serve immediately.

Cauliflower Scramble

Scrambled eggs are classic breakfast dish enjoyed by many. When you want to focus on plant-based foods, you can use cauliflower instead of eggs to create a scrumptious dish.

Time	30 minutes
Serving Size	3 servings
Prep Time	10 minutes
Cook Time	20 minutes

Nutritional Facts:
Calories: 89 kcal
Carbs: 16.8 grams
Fat: 0.8 grams
Protein: 7.6 grams

Ingredients:

- ⅛ tsp cayenne pepper
- ¼ tsp black pepper
- ¾ tsp turmeric
- 1 tbsp soy sauce (preferably low-sodium)
- ⅛ cup of nutritional yeast
- 1 cup of mushrooms (sliced)
- 2 cups of cauliflower florets
- ½ green bell pepper (seeds removed, diced)
- ½ red bell pepper (seeds removed, diced)
- ½ red onion (diced)
- 2 cloves of garlic (peeled, minced)
- Sea salt

Directions:

1. In a skillet, add the mushrooms, onion, green bell pepper, and red bell pepper over medium-high heat. Sauté for about 7 to 8 minutes. You may add some water if the veggies start sticking to the pan.
2. Add the cauliflower florets. Mix well and cook for about 5 to 6 minutes.
3. Add turmeric, soy sauce, cayenne, nutritional yeast, garlic, salt, and pepper. Cook for about 5 more minutes.
4. Spoon the cauliflower and scramble into plates.
5. Serve while hot.

Fully—Loaded Oatmeal

If you want something that will fill you up, this is an excellent choice. It's simple, nutritious, and takes very little time to prepare. You can even add different toppings to make an even tastier treat.

Time	15 minutes
Serving Size	1 serving
Prep Time	5 minutes
Cook Time	10 minutes

Nutritional Facts:
Calories: 458 kcal
Carbs: 76.7 grams
Fat: 13.6 grams
Protein: 13.3 grams

Ingredients:

- ¼ tsp cinnamon (ground)
- 2 tbsp raisins (you can also use other dried fruit like cranberries)
- 2 tbsp walnuts (chopped, you can also use cashews or pecans)
- ¼ cup of blueberries (fresh)
- ¾ cup of rolled oats
- 1 ½ cups of water
- ½ banana (sliced)
- A pinch of salt
- Apricots (sliced, for serving)
- Maple syrup (for serving)

Directions:

1. In a pot, add the water and oats over high heat. Bring to a boil.
2. Once boiling, turn the heat down to medium-low. Cook for about 5 minutes until the oats have absorbed all of the water.
3. Add the salt and cinnamon. Mix well.
4. Pour the oatmeal into a bowl.
5. Top with raisins, walnuts, sliced bananas, and apricots.
6. Drizzle the oatmeal with maple syrup
7. Serve while hot.

Crustless Quiche

This mouth-watering quiche contains the perfect combination of ingredients to create a winning dish. It's high in protein, low in cholesterol, and full of scrumptious flavors.

Time	1 hour, 20 minutes
Serving Size	2 servings
Prep Time	20 minutes
Cook Time	1 hour

Nutritional Facts:
Calories: 207 kcal
Carbs: 28.1 grams
Fat: 5.2 grams
Protein: 19 grams

Ingredients:

- ¼ tsp sea salt
- ¼ tsp turmeric
- ½ tsp hot sauce
- 1 tsp yellow mustard
- ½ tbsp cornstarch
- ½ tbsp tahini
- 1 tbsp vegetable broth (preferably low-sodium)
- 1 ½ tbsp lemon juice (freshly squeezed)
- 1 ½ tbsp nutritional yeast
- ⅛ cup of old-fashioned oats
- ¼ cup of artichoke hearts (chopped)
- ⅓ cup of sun-dried tomatoes (soaked in hot water)
- ¾ cup of broccoli florets
- ¾ cup of silken tofu (extra-firm, drained, dried)
- 1 clove of garlic (chopped)
- 1 leek (rinsed, sliced)
- Cooking spray

Directions:

1. Preheat your oven to 375°F. Use cooking spray to lightly grease a springform pan or pie plate.
2. On a baking sheet, add the broccoli florets, leeks, water, vegetable broth, salt,

and pepper. Toss well to coat the veggies.

3. Place the baking sheet in the oven. Bake the vegetables for about 25 to 30 minutes.

4. After baking, take the baking sheet out of the oven. Allow the veggies to cool down.

5. In a food processor, add the garlic, tofu, mustard, tahini, lemon juice, cornstarch, tabasco sauce, nutritional yeast, salt, and half of the oats. Blend everything together until smooth. Add more oats for a thicker texture.

6. In a bowl, add the artichoke hearts, tomatoes, baked veggies, and the oat mixture. Mix well. Add more vegetable broth if the mixture is too dry.

7. Transfer the mixture to the springform pan. Smoothen the top to create an even layer.

8. Place the springform pan in the oven. Bake the quiche for about 30 to 25 minutes.

9. Take the springform pan out of the oven.

10. Allow the quiche to cool down slightly before slicing and serving.

Acai Smoothie Bowl

Smoothie bowls are very nutritious and fun to eat. This recipe makes a tasty smoothie bowl with amazing tropical flavors that blend together wonderfully.

Time	5 minutes
Serving Size	1 serving
Prep Time	5 minutes
Cook Time	no cooking time

Nutritional Facts:
Calories: 249 kcal
Carbs: 63.9 grams
Fat: 0.8 grams
Protein: 2.3 grams

Ingredients:

- 1 tbsp lime juice (freshly squeezed)
- ¼ cup of water (cold)
- ½ cup of mango (frozen, diced)
- ¾ cup of acai pulp (unsweetened, frozen, thawed but not melted)
- 1 cup of pineapple chunks (frozen)
- 1 large banana (sliced)
- Toppings like strawberry slices, almond butter, blueberries, fresh mango cubes, fresh mint leaves, or large coconut flakes

Directions:

1. In a blender, add the acai pulp, water, lime juice, frozen mango, banana, and pineapple. Blend everything together until smooth.
2. Pour the mixture into a bowl.
3. Top with a dollop of almond butter and other desired toppings.
4. Serve immediately.

One—Skillet Savory Breakfast

This delicious plant-based breakfast is easy to prepare and easy to clean up too. It's a quick breakfast treat you can even serve when you invite guests over to your house.

Time	55 minutes
Serving Size	3 servings
Prep Time	35 minutes
Cook Time	20 minutes

Nutritional Facts:
Calories: 200 kcal
Carbs: 27 grams
Fat: 9 grams
Protein: 5 grams

Ingredients for the tofu scramble:

- ⅛ tsp black salt (kala namak)
- ⅛ tsp turmeric
- ¼ tsp black pepper
- ½ block of tofu (extra-firm, crumbled)

Ingredients for the rest of the ingredients:

- ⅛ tsp salt
- ½ tsp garlic powder
- ½ tsp pepper
- ¾ tsp Italian seasoning
- 1 tbsp maple syrup
- ⅛ cup of vegan butter (you can also use coconut oil)
- ⅛ cup of vegan cheese (shredded)
- ¼ cup of baby Bella mushrooms (diced)
- ½ cup of spinach
- ¼ green pepper (seeds removed, sliced)
- ¼ orange pepper (seeds removed, sliced)
- ¼ red pepper (seeds removed, sliced)
- ¼ sweet onion (sliced)
- ¼ yellow pepper (seeds removed, sliced)
- 2 Yukon potatoes (rinsed, cubed, soaked in water for half an hour)
- Toppings like salsa or mashed avocado
- ¼ lb vegan sausage (optional, crumbled)

Directions:

1. In a skillet, add coconut oil over medium-

high heat.

2. Add the potatoes and arrange them in one layer.

3. Cook for about 2 minutes, then flip them over. Cook for 2 minutes more. Repeat this step for about 10 minutes.

4. Turn the heat down to medium-low. Add the onions and peppers, then mix well.

5. If you want to add vegan sausage, do so here. Cook for about 4 minutes. If not, skip this step.

6. Add the Italian seasoning, garlic powder, salt, and pepper. Mix well.

7. Push the vegetable mixture to one side of the skillet. Add the tofu to the other side along with the black salt, turmeric, and pepper.

8. Scramble the tofu for about 2 to 3 minutes.

9. Mix all the scrambled tofu with the cooked veggies.

10. Add the mushrooms and spinach. Cook for about 2 minutes.

11. Add the maple syrup and vegan cheese. Mix well.

12. Spoon the mixture into three plates.

13. Top each plate with mashed avocado, salsa, or any other desired toppings.

14. Serve immediately.

CHAPTER 4
LIGHT AND SIMPLE SOUPS, SALADS, AND APPETIZERS

Before enjoying a meal, you may want to have a light soup, salad, or appetizer first. In this chapter, you will learn how to create amazingly healthy and mouth-watering plant-based dishes to start off your meals.

Vegetable Soup With Turmeric

This comforting soup dish contains turmeric, one of the healthiest spices on the planet. It's also considered an economical dish since it contains a mixture of very cheap ingredients to create a satisfying dish.

Time	35 minutes
Serving Size	3 servings
Prep Time	10 minutes
Cook Time	25 minutes

Nutritional Facts:

Calories: 260 kcal
Carbs: 54 grams
Fat: 2 grams
Protein: 12 grams

Ingredients:

- ½ tsp black pepper
- ½ tsp coriander seeds
- 1 tsp salt
- 1 tsp turmeric
- 2 tsp cumin
- 2 tsp sweet paprika
- 1 tbsp ginger (grated)
- 1 tbsp lemon juice (freshly squeezed)
- 1 tbsp tomato paste
- 2 tbsp water
- 1 cup of red lentils
- 1 cup of tomatoes (canned, diced)
- 2 cups of baby spinach
- 1 bunch of parsley (finely chopped)
- 1 large yellow onion (finely chopped)
- 1 Russet potato (peeled, cubed)
- 2 carrots (peeled, sliced thinly)
- 3 cloves of garlic (diced)
- 3 stalks of celery (diced)
- 4 cups of vegetable broth (homemade or store-bought, preferably low-sodium)

Directions:

1. In a pot, add the potato, onion, garlic, celery, carrot, coriander seeds, turmeric, cumin, ginger, paprika, salt, pepper, and water over medium heat. Sauté for about 5 minutes.

2. Add the tomatoes, vegetable broth, and tomato paste. Stir everything together, then bring the mixture to a boil.

3. Once boiling, add the lentils. Mix well, then turn the heat down to low.

4. Allow simmering for about 15 minutes.

5. Add the spinach. Continue cooking for about 5 minutes more.

6. Take the pot off the heat.

7. Add the lemon juice and parsley, then mix well.

8. Serve while hot.

Hearty Potato Soup

This is a simple soup dish but the result is amazing! It's creamy, comforting, and contains just the right combination of ingredients to make you feel happy and satisfied.

Time	40 minutes
Serving Size	3 servings
Prep Time	10 minutes
Cook Time	30 minutes

Nutritional Facts:
Calories: 238 kcal
Carbs: 34 grams
Fat: 8 grams
Protein: 9 grams

Ingredients:

- ⅛ tsp black pepper
- ½ tsp salt
- 1 tbsp vegan butter
- 1 ½ tbsp vegan broth base
- ⅛ cup of nutritional yeast flakes
- ¼ cup of cashews (raw)
- ½ cup of onions (chopped)
- 2 ½ cups of water
- 1 small bay leaf
- 1 stalk of celery (chopped)
- 2 cloves of garlic (finely chopped)
- 3 potatoes (rinsed, cubed)

Directions:

1. In a microwave-safe bowl, add the water. Heat for about 5 to 6 minutes until the water is about to boil.
2. Add the broth base and cashews. Mix well and allow to sit for about 10 minutes in the microwave.
3. In a pot, add butter over medium heat.
4. Once the butter has melted, add the celery and onions. Cook for about 2 to 3 minutes.
5. Add the potatoes. Cook for about 5 to 7 minutes while stirring occasionally.
6. In the meantime, add the water mixture to a blender along with the nutritional

yeast. Blend for a couple of seconds to pulverize the cashews and create a mixture that looks like milk.

7. Add the mixture to the pot along with the bay leaf. Stir everything together and bring the mixture to a boil.

8. Once boiling, turn the heat down to low. Allow simmering for about 20 to 25 minutes until the potatoes are fork-tender.

9. Take the bay leaf out. Use a potato masher to mash the potatoes roughly for a chunky texture.

10. Season with salt and pepper, then mix everything together. Allow the soup to sit for about 10 minutes to thicken.

11. Serve while warm with your choice of toppings like bacon bits, croutons, or crackers on the side.

Fully—Loaded Minestrone Soup

Here's another cozy and tasty soup recipe for you. Minestrone is a classic dish that will warm you up on cold days or nights.

Time	1 hour
Serving Size	4 servings
Prep Time	20 minutes
Cook Time	40 minutes

Nutritional Facts:
Calories: 308 kcal
Carbs: 53.8 grams
Fat: 5.9 grams
Protein: 14 grams

Ingredients:

- ¼ tsp red pepper flakes
- 1 tsp thyme (fresh, minced)
- ½ tbsp olive oil
- ½ tbsp sage (fresh, minced)
- ½ tbsp tomato paste
- ¼ cup of orzo pasta (you can also use other types of dry, small pasta)
- 1 cup of chickpeas (canned, rinsed, drained)
- 1 ½ cups of butternut squash (peeled, diced)
- 1 ¾ cup of tomatoes (canned, crushed)
- 3 ½ cups of vegetable stock (homemade or store-bought)
- 1 small bunch of chard (chopped)
- 1 small carrot (peeled, diced)
- 1 small yellow onion (diced)
- 1 small zucchini (diced)
- 2 garlic cloves (minced)
- Black pepper
- Sea salt

Directions:

1. In a pot, add olive oil over medium-high heat.
2. Once the oil is hot enough, add the carrots and onions. Sauté for about 3 minutes.

3. Add the thyme, red pepper flakes, tomato paste, sage, and garlic. Mix well and cook for about 30 seconds.

4. Add the chickpeas, butternut squash, zucchini, salt, and pepper. Mix everything together until well combined.

5. Add the vegetable stock and tomatoes. Stir everything together, then bring the mixture to a boil.

6. Once boiling, turn the heat down to low. Allow simmering for about 20 to 23 minutes until the butternut squash is fork-tender.

7. Add the orzo pasta. Continue simmering for about 10 minutes.

8. Add the chard and continue simmering for about 2 minutes.

9. Serve while hot.

Cauliflower and Leek Soup

This creamy soup is completely nu and dairy-free. It's a one-pot recipe that you can cook in just 35 minutes making it the perfect choice even if you have a busy schedule.

Time	35 minutes
Serving Size	3 servings
Prep Time	10 minutes
Cook Time	25 minutes

Nutritional Facts:
Calories: 83 kcal
Carbs: 14 grams
Fat: 2 grams
Protein: 5 grams

Ingredients:

- ½ tsp thyme (dried)
- ¾ tsp garlic powder
- ¾ tsp onion powder
- 1 tbsp nutritional yeast
- 3 cups of vegetable broth (homemade or store-bought)
- 1 bay leaf
- 1 cauliflower head (roughly chopped)
- 1 leek (top and roots removed, sliced thinly)
- Himalayan pink salt
- Pepper
- Toppings like shredded vegan cheese, coconut bacon, or sliced green onion

Directions:

1. In a soup pot, add all of the ingredients over medium-high heat. Mix all of the ingredients together, then bring to a boil.
2. Once boiling, turn the heat down to medium. Cover the soup pot and simmer for about 20 to 25 minutes until the cauliflower is fork-tender.
3. Pour the soup into a blender. Blend until creamy and smooth.
4. Prepare three bowls and divide the soup into them.
5. Serve while hot with toppings of your choice.

Classic Tomato Soup

Let this classic dish warm you up after a long, hard day. It's another easy recipe for you to make at home. It's nutritious, tasty, and super comforting too.

Time	25 minutes
Serving Size	2 servings
Prep Time	5 minutes
Cook Time	20 minutes

Nutritional Facts:
Calories: 229 kcal
Carbs: 16 grams
Fat: 18 grams
Protein: 1 gram

Ingredients:

- 1 tbsp brown sugar
- 4 tbsp vegan butter
- ½ cup of cannellini beans (cooked, you can also use chickpeas)
- 1 cup of onion (roughly chopped)
- 1 ½ cups of vegetable broth (homemade or store-bought)
- 3 ¾ cups of tomatoes (canned, peeled, crushed, or whole)
- 1 clove of garlic (roughly chopped)
- Toppings like vegan cream, croutons, or vegan Parmesan

Directions:

1. In a saucepan, add the butter over medium heat.
2. Once the butter has melted, add the onion. Cook for about 1 to 2 minutes.
3. Add the brown sugar and garlic. Cook for about 1 minute.
4. Add the vegetable broth and tomatoes (along with the juices). Stir everything together, then bring the mixture to a boil.
5. Once boiling, turn the heat down to low. Allow simmering for about 20 minutes.
6. Add the cannellini beans and mix well.
7. Pour the mixture into a blender. Blend until creamy and smooth.

8. Prepare two bowls and divide the soup between them.
9. Top with toppings of your choice.
10. Serve while hot.

Quinoa and Black Bean Salad

Most people only think of salads when they hear about plant-based diets. While you will be eating a lot of salads when you go plant-based, that doesn't mean your diet won't be interesting. Here's a filling and mouth-watering salad recipe to start you off.

Time	30 minutes
Serving Size	3 servings
Prep Time	15 minutes
Cook Time	15 minutes

Nutritional Facts:
Calories: 454 kcal
Carbs: 56.1 grams
Fat: 22.4 grams
Protein: 13.4 grams

Ingredients for the salad:

- ¼ tsp oregano
- ⅛ cup of red onion (finely chopped)
- ¼ cup of cilantro (fresh, chopped)
- ¼ cup of scallions (sliced)
- ⅓ cup of quinoa (dry, rinsed, drained)
- ½ cup of water
- ¾ cup of black beans (cooked)
- ¾ cup of corn (charred)
- ¾ cups of tomatoes (diced)
- 1 avocado (seed removed, cut into cubes)

Ingredients for the dressing:

- ⅛ tsp chipotle powder
- ⅛ tsp smoked paprika
- ¼ tsp chili powder
- ¼ tsp coriander
- ¼ tsp pepper
- ½ tsp cumin (ground)
- ½ tsp fine sea salt
- ½ tsp maple syrup
- 2 tsp lime zest
- 1 ½ tbsp extra-virgin olive oil
- ⅛ cup of lime juice (freshly squeezed)
- 1 clove of garlic (finely minced)

Directions:

1. In a bowl, add all of the dressing

ingredients. Mix well and set aside.

2. In a pot, add water with the oregano and quinoa over medium heat. Bring to a simmer.

3. Once simmering, cover the pot and cook the quinoa for about 15 minutes.

4. Allow the quinoa to cool down for about 5 to 10 minutes before fluffing with a fork.

5. While the quinoa cools down, prepare the other ingredients.

6. In a bowl, add the tomatoes, corn, black beans, red onion, scallions, and cilantro. Toss to combine.

7. Add the quinoa and toss well.

8. Drizzle the dressing into the bowl, then toss well.

9. Top with avocado cubes and serve immediately.

Roasted Veggie Salad

This recipe features perfectly roasted veggies with a tangy dressing that complements the salad wonderfully. It's a colorful fall salad that's refreshing and hearty at the same time.

Time	50 minutes
Serving Size	2 servings
Prep Time	25 minutes
Cook Time	25 minutes

Nutritional Facts:
Calories: 578 kcal
Carbs: 72 grams
Fat: 30 grams
Protein: 16 grams

Ingredients for the salad:

- ¼ tsp red pepper flakes
- ½ tsp cumin (ground)
- ½ tbsp maple syrup
- 1 tbsp extra virgin olive oil
- 1 cup of chickpeas (canned, rinsed, drained)
- 2 cups of kale (chopped)
- ½ small butternut squash (seeds removed, peeled, thinly sliced)
- ½ small green cabbage (sliced into thick wedges)
- 2 carrots (peeled, cut into thin ribbons)
- Black pepper
- Kosher salt

Ingredients for the dressing:

- ¼ tsp red pepper flakes
- ⅓ tsp Dijon mustard
- ⅓ tsp oregano (dried)
- 1 tsp maple syrup
- 1 ½ tbsp extra virgin olive oil
- 1 ½ tbsp red wine vinegar
- 2 cloves of garlic (finely minced)

Ingredients for the topping:

- 1 tbsp agave nectar
- ¼ cup of almonds (whole, unsalted)

- A pinch of cayenne pepper
- Kosher salt

Directions:

1. In a bowl, add all of the dressing ingredients. Mix well and set aside.
2. Preheat your oven to 450°F.
3. On a rimmed baking sheet, add the cabbage wedges.
4. Sprinkle with salt and pepper, then drizzle with ½ tablespoon of olive oil. Use your hands to rub the seasonings and oil all over the cabbage leaves.
5. Move the seasoned cabbage leaves to one side of the baking sheet.
6. In a bowl, add the squash slices, maple syrup, red pepper flakes, salt, pepper, and the rest of the olive oil. Toss to coat the squash slices.
7. Add the slices to the other side of the baking sheet and arrange them in one layer.
8. Place the baking sheet in the oven. Roast the vegetables for about 25 minutes. After about 12 minutes, take the baking sheet out. Flip the squash slices over and toss the cabbage leaves around.
9. While roasting the veggies, prepare the topping. Use a sheet of paper to line a

plate.

10. Heat a pan over medium heat.

11. Once the pan is hot enough, add all of the topping ingredients.

12. Cook for about 2 to 3 minutes while stirring constantly.

13. Transfer the almond toppings to the plate and arrange them in a pile.

14. Allow to cool down for a few minutes for the almonds to stick to each other.

15. When cool enough to handle, break the almond pile into small clumps.

16. After roasting, take the baking sheet out of the oven.

17. In a bowl, add the carrots, chickpeas, and kale. Toss well.

18. Add the roasted veggies and dressing, then toss well to combine.

19. Top the salad with the crunchy almonds and serve.

Zesty Caesar Salad

This easy salad is fresh, crunchy, and super healthy. It takes the classic Caesar salad to the next level without the addition of any animal-based ingredients.

Time	5 minutes
Serving Size	2 servings
Prep Time	5 minutes
Cook Time	no cooking time

Nutritional Facts:
Calories: 392 kcal
Carbs: 64.1 grams
Fat: 12.4 grams
Protein: 11.6 grams

Ingredients for the salad:

- 2 tbsp nutritional yeast
- 1 cup of carrots (peeled, shredded)
- 1 cup of parsley (fresh, roughly chopped)
- 2 heads of romaine lettuce hearts (rinsed, dried, chopped)
- 2 sweet potatoes (peeled, roasted, roughly chopped)

Ingredients for the dressing:

- ½ tsp lemon zest
- 1 tsp olive oil
- 1 ½ tsp spicy mustard
- 2 tsp brining juice of capers
- 2 tsp capers (chopped)
- 2 tsp maple syrup
- 2 tbsp lemon juice (freshly squeezed)
- ½ cup of hummus (plain, homemade, or store-bought)
- 4 cloves of garlic (minced)
- A pinch of pepper
- A pinch of sea salt

Directions:

1. In a bowl, add all of the dressing ingredients. Mix well.
2. In a bowl, add the parsley, carrots, and lettuce. Toss well.

3. Drizzle with the dressing and toss well to combine.
4. Transfer the salad to a serving platter.
5. Top with roasted sweet potatoes, then sprinkle with nutritional yeast.
6. Serve immediately.

Asian—Style Salad With Soba Noodles

If you're looking for a unique salad, here is one for you to try. This Asian-style dish includes soba noodles making it hearty and satisfying.

Time	15 minutes
Serving Size	2 servings
Prep Time	9 minutes
Cook Time	6 minutes

Nutritional Facts:
Calories: 396 kcal
Carbs: 66 grams
Fat: 10.2 grams
Protein: 17.4 grams

Ingredients for the salad:

- 2 tsp sugar
- 1 tbsp mirin
- 2 tbsp toasted sesame oil
- ¼ cup of rice wine vinegar
- ¼ cup of soy sauce

Ingredients for the dressing:

- 2 tbsp sesame seeds (toasted)
- ½ cup of green onion (finely chopped)
- ½ cup of tofu (cubed, baked)
- 1 cup of buckwheat soba noodles
- 1 cup of mixed herbs like cilantro, mint, and dill (roughly chopped)
- 1 cup of snow peas (chopped)
- 1 ½ cups of cucumber (diced)
- 2 cups of green cabbage (shredded)
- 1 bell pepper (seeds removed, sliced into strips)
- A pinch of salt
- Water (for cooking the soba noodles)

Directions:

1. In a bowl, add all of the dressing ingredients. Mix well and set aside.
2. In a pot, add water and salt over medium heat. Bring to a boil.
3. Once boiling, add the soba noodles. Cook

for about 4 to 6 minutes.

4. After cooking, drain the water and rinse the noodles. Transfer the noodles to a bowl.

5. Add the vegetables to the bowl, then toss to combine.

6. Drizzle the dressing over the salad and toss well.

7. Top with baked tofu and sprinkle with sesame seeds.

8. Serve immediately.

Herbed Potato Salad

This potato salad takes the classic dish to a new level by making it more flavorful. This salad is mayonnaise free and yet it's still tangy and creamy at the same time.

Time	15 minutes
Serving Size	4 servings
Prep Time	5 minutes
Cook Time	10 minutes

Nutritional Facts:
Calories: 196 kcal
Carbs: 32 grams
Fat: 6 grams
Protein: 6 grams

Ingredients for the salad:

- 1 tbsp capers (drained)
- 1 tbsp chives (fresh, chopped)
- ¼ cup of red onions (thinly sliced)
- 1 small jalapeño pepper (seeds removed, thinly sliced)
- Flaky sea salt
- 1 ¼ cups of baby red potatoes (scrubbed well, cut in half, you can also use new potatoes or fingerling potatoes)
- Water (for boiling the potatoes)

Ingredients for the dressing:

- ½ tsp celery seeds
- ½ tsp kosher salt
- 1 tsp Dijon mustard
- 1 tsp yellow mustard
- 1 ½ tsp lemon zest
- ½ tbsp caper brine
- 1 ½ tbsp lemon juice (freshly squeezed)
- ⅛ cup of tahini
- ¼ cup of coconut yogurt (unsweetened)
- ⅓ cup of dill leaves (fresh, finely chopped)
- 1 clove of garlic (finely minced)
- Black pepper

Directions:

1. In a bowl, add all of the dressing ingredients. Mix well and set aside.
2. In a pot filled with cold water and a pinch of salt, add the potatoes over medium heat. Make sure all of the potatoes are submerged in the water. Bring to a simmer.
3. Continue simmering for about 8 to 10 minutes until the potatoes are fork-tender.
4. Drain the water using a colander.
5. Leave the potatoes in the colander for about 5 minutes.
6. Transfer the potatoes to a bowl and drizzle the dressing over them. Toss well to coat all of the potatoes.
7. Add the jalapeño, capers, and red onions. Toss gently to combine everything.
8. Sprinkle chives and dill over the salad.
9. Serve immediately or chill in the refrigerator before serving.

Eggplant Rolls

This first appetizer recipe is truly a winner. These eggplant rolls are delightfully simple, healthy, and tasty. The spices work perfectly together to create amazing flavors.

Time	40 minutes
Serving Size	5 servings
Prep Time	10 minutes
Cook Time	30 minutes

Nutritional Facts:
Calories: 46 kcal
Carbs: 4 grams
Fat: 3 grams
Protein: 1 gram

Ingredients:

- ½ tsp coriander (ground)
- ½ tsp khmeli suneli spice mix
- 1 tsp white wine vinegar
- ¼ cup of water (very hot)
- ¾ cup of walnuts (crushed)
- 1 clove of garlic (minced)
- 2 eggplants
- Black pepper
- Salt
- Cooking spray
- 1 ½ tbsp pomegranate seeds (for serving)

Directions:

1. Preheat your oven to 350°F. Use cooking spray to lightly grease a baking tray.
2. Use a sharp knife to slice off the tops of the eggplants.
3. Slice the eggplants lengthwise into long, thin strips, then place the eggplant strips on the baking tray.
4. Lightly grease the tops of the eggplant slices. Season with salt and pepper.
5. Place the baking tray in the oven. Bake the eggplant slices for about 30 minutes. After about 15 minutes, flip the eggplant slices over.
6. While the eggplant slices are baking, prepare the filling. In a bowl, add the

walnuts, khmeli suneli, garlic, white wine vinegar, coriander, salt, and pepper. Mix well.

7. Gradually add very hot water into the bowl while stirring the mixture constantly. Continue stirring and pouring water until you get the filling consistency you desire.

8. Take the baking tray out of the oven. Allow the eggplant slices to cool down a bit.

9. Once cool enough to handle, add 1 heaping teaspoon of filling to the end of one eggplant slice.

10. Roll the eggplant slice and place on a plate.

11. Repeat the assembling steps for the remaining eggplant rolls.

12. Sprinkle pomegranate seeds over the eggplant rolls.

13. Serve while hot.

Savory Flatbread

This recipe is quick and easy, and you can customize it using different ingredients. It's a flavorful dish that you can enjoy at any time of the day.

Time	30 minutes
Serving Size	1 serving
Prep Time	15 minutes
Cook Time	15 minutes

Nutritional Facts:

Calories: 492 kcal
Carbs: 35.1 grams
Fat: 37.1 grams
Protein: 15.3 grams

Ingredients:

- 2 tbsp parsley (fresh, chopped)
- 2 tbsp pine nuts
- 3 tbsp tahini
- 3 cloves of garlic (minced)
- 2 ¼ cups of cherry tomatoes and regular tomatoes (mixed, sliced)
- 350 grams of pizza dough (homemade or store-bought)
- Pepper
- Salt
- Cooking spray

Directions:

1. Preheat your oven to 480°F. Use cooking spray to lightly grease a baking sheet.
2. Roll the pizza dough into the shape you desire and place it on a baking sheet.
3. Spread the tahini all over the flatbread.
4. Sprinkle with garlic, then season with salt and pepper.
5. Arrange the sliced tomatoes on the flatbread, then add the pine nuts.
6. Place the baking sheet in the oven. Bake the flatbread for about 15 to 20 minutes.
7. Take the baking sheet out of the oven.
8. Sprinkle parsley all over the flatbread and serve while hot.

Cauliflower Buffalo Bites

Buffalo wings are a very popular appetizer. Since you are on a plant-based diet, you can make your own version of buffalo wings using fresh cauliflower.

Time	40 minutes
Serving Size	3 servings
Prep Time	5 minutes
Cook Time	35 minutes

Nutritional Facts:
Calories: 144 kcal
Carbs: 21 grams
Fat: 5 grams
Protein: 5 grams

Ingredients for the cauliflower bites:

- ½ tsp baking powder
- ½ tsp garlic powder
- ½ tsp onion powder
- ½ tsp salt
- 1 tsp hot sauce
- 1 tsp oil
- 3 tbsp cornstarch
- ¼ cup of all-purpose flour
- ⅓ cup of almond milk (you can also use soy milk)
- 4 cups of cauliflower (florets)
- Cooking spray

Ingredients for the sauce:

- ½ tsp cayenne pepper
- ½ tsp garlic powder
- ½ tsp herb seasoning (combine ¼ tsp sage and ¼ tsp onion powder)
- 1 tsp black pepper
- 1 tsp sugar (you can also use maple syrup)
- 1 tsp sweet paprika
- 1 tbsp oil
- 1 tbsp vinegar
- 1 tbsp water
- 2 tbsp hot sauce

Directions:

1. Preheat your oven to 425°F. Use parchment paper to line a baking dish.

2. In a bowl, add all of the cauliflower ingredients except for the cauliflower florets. Whisk well.

3. Add the cauliflower florets to the bowl. Toss well to coat all of the pieces.

4. Transfer the cauliflower bites to a baking dish. Arrange them in one layer, then lightly grease the surface with cooking spray.

5. Place the baking dish in the oven. Bake the cauliflower bites for about 25 minutes.

6. While baking the cauliflower bites, prepare the sauce. In a bowl, add all of the sauce ingredients. Mix well and set aside.

7. Take the baking dish out of the oven. Allow the cauliflower bites to cool down for about 5 minutes.

8. Add the cauliflower bites to the bowl with the sauce. Toss to coat all of the pieces.

9. Transfer the buffalo cauliflower bites back to the baking dish and turn the heat down to 400°F.

10. Place the baking dish back in the oven. Bake the buffalo cauliflower bites for

about 15 minutes.

11. After baking, take the baking dish out of the oven.

12. Serve the cauliflower bites while hot with a vegan dipping sauce of your choice.

Sweet and Savory Rolls

These freshly baked rolls make a wonderful appetizer. You can even enjoy them as a light meal. The recipe even comes with a flavorful sauce for dipping.

Time	25 minutes
Serving Size	2 servings
Prep Time	25 minutes
Cook Time	no cooking time

Nutritional Facts:
Calories: 433 kcal
Carbs: 41.6 grams
Fat: 21.9 grams
Protein: 8.5 grams

Ingredients for the sauce:

- ⅛ tsp sea salt
- ¼ tsp ginger (fresh, chopped)
- ½ tbsp cashew butter
- ⅛ tbsp lime juice (freshly squeezed)
- ⅛ cup of basil
- ¼ cup of coconut milk (preferably full-fat)
- ¼ small jalapeño (seeds removed, sliced)
- ½ clove of garlic
- Water (warm)

Ingredients for the rolls:

- ¼ cup of rice noodles (cooked)
- ¼ cup of tofu (extra-firm, sliced into strips)
- ¼ watermelon radish (very thinly sliced)
- ½ avocado (sliced)
- 1 peach (sliced)
- 4 spring roll rice wrappers
- A pinch of sesame seeds (for serving)
- Basil (fresh, for serving)
- Sriracha (for serving)

Directions:

1. In a food processor, add all of the sauce ingredients. Pulse until smooth.
2. Pour the sauce into a bowl and set aside.

3. Pour some warm water into a shallow dish.
4. Place one rice paper roll into the dish and soak it for about 7 seconds.
5. Transfer the rice paper roll to a damp and clean kitchen towel.
6. In the middle of the rice paper roll, arrange the fillings.
7. Take the bottom of the wrapper and fold it to the middle. Fold the sides to the middle, then roll it from the bottom.
8. Dampen the top of the rice paper roll with warm water to seal it.
9. Repeat the assembling steps for the remaining rolls.
10. Sprinkle the rolls with basil and sesame seeds, then drizzle with sriracha.
11. Serve immediately with dipping sauce on the side.

Jalapeño Poppers

These jalapeño poppers are crunchy on the outside and creamy on the inside. Have them as an appetizer before your meal or as a light and savory snack.

Time	25 minutes
Serving Size	4 servings
Prep Time	15 minutes
Cook Time	40 minutes

Nutritional Facts:
Calories: 331 kcal
Carbs: 15 grams
Fat: 29 grams
Protein: 2 grams

Ingredients for the jalapeños:

- ½ tbsp nutritional yeast
- ¼ cup of aquafaba
- ⅓ cup of cornflour (you can also use cornstarch)
- ½ cup of white rice flour
- 1 ½ cups of vegetable oil
- 8 jalapeños

Ingredients for the filling:

- ¼ tsp salt
- ½ tbsp garlic powder
- 1 ½ tbsp nutritional yeast
- ⅛ cup of water
- ½ cup of cashew nuts (raw, soaked overnight)

Directions:

1. In a blender, add all of the filling ingredients. Blend until creamy.
2. Scoop the filling into a bowl and set aside.
3. Use a sharp knife to slice a lengthwise T-shape in the middle of the jalapeños.
4. Use a teaspoon to scoop out the flesh and seeds.
5. Fill each of the jalapeños with 1 teaspoon of filling.
6. In a bowl, add the aquafaba.

7. In a shallow dish, add the cornflour, rice flour, and nutritional yeast. Mix well.

8. Dip one jalapeño in the aquafaba making sure to coat it completely.

9. Dip the jalapeño in the shallow dish and coat with the flour mixture. Place the coated jalapeño on a plate.

10. Repeat the coating steps for the rest of the jalapeños.

11. In a pot, add vegetable oil over medium-high heat.

12. Once the oil is hot enough, add the jalapeño poppers. Cook for about 3 to 4 minutes until crispy and golden brown.

13. Transfer the cooked jalapeño poppers to a plate lined with a paper towel.

14. Serve while hot with a vegan dipping sauce of your choice.

CHAPTER 5
MOUTH-WATERING MAIN COURSE RECIPES FOR LUNCH AND DINNER

After a scrumptious appetizer, it's time to enjoy your main course. In this chapter, you will learn how to make several dishes that you can eat for lunch or dinner. As you will soon realize, going plant-based means having an interesting, diverse, and nutritious diet. These dishes are easy to make yet the results are unbelievably flavorful.

Green Alfredo Pasta

Alfredo pasta is a very popular dish. Usually, it's made with cream, milk, and chicken or bacon. For this version, you will make green alfredo pasta for your plant-based diet.

Time	10 minutes
Serving Size	2 servings
Prep Time	10 minutes
Cook Time	no cooking time

Nutritional Facts:
Calories: 354 kcal
Carbs: 42 grams
Fat: 16 grams
Protein: 19 grams

Ingredients:

- 1 tsp onion powder
- 1 tbsp lemon zest
- 3 tbsp lemon juice (freshly squeezed)
- ¼ cup of almond milk (you can also use any other dairy-free milk)
- ¼ cup of nutritional yeast
- ½ cup of basil leaves (fresh)
- ½ cup of butter beans
- ½ cup of cashews (raw, soaked overnight)
- 1 cup of cherry tomatoes (cut in half)
- 1 clove of garlic
- 2 zucchinis (spiralized or sliced into zoodles)
- A pinch of salt

Directions:

1. In a bowl, add the zucchini and ¾ cup of cherry tomatoes. Toss to combine, then set aside.
2. In a blender, add the rest of the ingredients, except for the remaining tomatoes. Blend until smooth. If needed, add some water to help with the blending process.
3. Pour the sauce into the bowl and toss to coat.
4. Prepare two plates and divide the pasta

between them.

5. Top with the rest of the tomatoes and serve immediately.

Meatless Beef Stew

If you're craving a cozy and filling meal, whip up this dish for yourself. It's chunky, flavorful, and has a wonderful meaty texture thanks to the portobello mushrooms.

Time	45 minutes
Serving Size	4 servings
Prep Time	10 minutes
Cook Time	35 minutes

Nutritional Facts:
Calories: 250 kcal
Carbs: 52.9 grams
Fat: 1.7 grams
Protein: 9.2 grams

Ingredients:

- 1 tsp rosemary (fresh, finely chopped)
- ½ tbsp Italian seasoning
- ½ tbsp paprika
- 1 tbsp water
- ¼ cup of parsley (fresh, chopped)
- ¼ cup of tomato paste (no-salt-added)
- ½ cup of celery (sliced)
- ¾ cup of peas (frozen, thawed)
- 1 cup of carrots (peeled, sliced lengthwise, cut into strips)
- 1 ½ cups of yellow onions (chopped)
- 3 cups of white potatoes (peeled, roughly chopped)
- 2 ½ cups of water
- 1 portobello mushroom (roughly chopped)
- 3 cloves of garlic (minced)

Directions:

1. In a soup pot, add the water, celery, onions, and carrots over medium-high heat. Cook for about 8 minutes while stirring frequently. If the veggies start sticking to the pot, add more water.

2. Add the garlic and mushrooms. Cook for about 5 minutes while stirring frequently. Continue adding water as needed.

3. Add the tomato paste, potatoes, Italian seasoning, and 2 ½ cups of water. Stir everything together. Bring the mixture to a boil.
4. Once boiling, turn the heat down to medium-low.
5. Add the rosemary, then cover the pot with a lid. Allow simmering for about 15 minutes while stirring occasionally.
6. Add the peas and stir well. Cook for about 5 minutes until the carrots and potatoes are fork-tender.
7. Pour half of the mixture into a blender. Blend until creamy and smooth.
8. Pour the soup back into the pot along with the parsley, then mix well.
9. Serve while hot.

Bright and Healthy Buddha Bowl

Buddha bowls are very popular these days. They are super easy to make and you can customize them however you wish. For this recipe, you will use different fresh veggies.

Time	35 minutes
Serving Size	2 servings
Prep Time	15 minutes
Cook Time	20 minutes

Nutritional Facts:
Calories: 623 kcal
Carbs: 120.1 grams
Fat: 8 grams
Protein: 19.7 grams

Ingredients:

- 2 tbsp lemon juice (freshly squeezed)
- 1 tbsp sesame seeds (you can also use hemp seeds)
- ⅓ cup of sauerkraut
- ½ cup of chickpeas (cooked, you can also use lentils)
- 1 cup of brown rice (cooked, you can also use quinoa)
- 1 cup of red cabbage (shredded)
- 2 cups of microgreens
- 1 carrot (peeled, sliced into ribbons)
- 1 sweet potato (rinsed, scrubbed, cut into cubes)
- 2 red radishes (peeled, thinly sliced)
- 4 kale leaves (tough parts removed)
- Black pepper
- Sea salt
- Extra-virgin olive oil (for drizzling)
- Tahini sauce (for serving)

Directions:

1. Preheat your oven to 400°F. Use parchment paper to line a baking sheet.
2. In a bowl, add the olive oil, sweet potatoes, salt, and pepper. Toss well to coat the sweet potato cubes.
3. Transfer the sweet potatoes to a baking sheet and arrange in one layer.

4. Place the baking sheet in the oven. Roast the sweet potatoes for about 20 minutes until golden brown.

5. While roasting the sweet potatoes, prepare the rest of the ingredients. In a bowl, add the cabbage, carrots, radishes, and half of the lemon juice. Toss to coat, then set aside.

6. In a separate bowl, add the kale, salt, and the rest of the lemon juice. Use your hands to gently massage the salt and lemon juice into the kale leaves.

7. After roasting the sweet potatoes, take the baking sheet out of the oven.

8. Prepare two bowls. In each bowl, add chickpeas, brown rice, two kale leaves, radishes, carrots, cabbage, sauerkraut, microgreens, and roasted sweet potatoes.

9. Sprinkle sesame seeds, salt, and pepper over each of the Buddha bowls.

10. Drizzle olive oil over each of the Buddha bowls.

11. Serve immediately with tahini sauce on the side.

Roasted Red Pepper and Pesto Sandwich

This sandwich is cheesy, creamy, and smoky. It has all the right flavors sealed within two pieces of bread. Enjoy it for lunch or dinner with your whole family.

Time	35 minutes (steaming time not included
Serving Size	4 servings
Prep Time	15 minutes
Cook Time	40 minutes

Nutritional Facts:
Calories: 376 kcal
Carbs: 48 grams
Fat: 16 grams
Protein: 13 grams

Ingredients:

- ⅛ cup of pesto (homemade or store-bought)
- 2 red bell peppers
- 4 slices of bread
- 8 slices of vegan mozzarella cheese
- Himalayan salt
- Pepper

Directions:

1. Set your oven to broil and place a rack on the highest level. Use aluminum foil to line a baking sheet.
2. Place the bell peppers on the baking sheet.
3. Place the baking sheet in the oven. Broil the bell peppers for about 20 minutes. Every 5 minutes or so, turn the bell peppers to make sure that all sides get charred.
4. Take the baking sheet out of the oven.
5. Place the bell peppers on a plate, then cover the plate with a bowl. Allow the bell peppers to steam in their own heat for about 13 to 15 minutes.
6. After steaming, remove the bowl. Transfer the bell peppers to a chopping board.
7. Use a knife to slice the bell peppers

vertically, then spread each of them open.

8. Remove the seeds and stems. Peel off the charred skin.
9. Slice the bell peppers into strips, then season with salt and pepper.
10. Spread pesto over each of the bread slices.
11. Top each bread slice with two slices of mozzarella cheese, then top with the bell pepper slices.
12. Put the bread slices on top of each other to make sandwiches.
13. Serve while hot.

Nacho Baked Potato

There is nothing more comforting than having a baked potato for lunch or dinner. This recipe makes the classic dish more interesting by adding nacho toppings to the mix!

Time	50 minutes
Serving Size	1 serving
Prep Time	10 minutes
Cook Time	40 minutes

Nutritional Facts:
Calories: 855 kcal
Carbs: 140 grams
Fat: 21.7 grams
Protein: 33.6 grams

Ingredients:

- 1 ½ tsp nutritional yeast
- ¼ cup salsa (homemade or store-bought)
- ½ cup of black beans (canned, rinsed, drained)
- ½ avocado (sliced, smashed, or cut into cubes)
- 1 large potato
- Black pepper
- Salt
- Cilantro (for garnish)
- Lime wedges (for garnish)

Directions:

1. Preheat your oven to 450°F.
2. Use a fork to poke holes all over the potato. Place the potato on a baking sheet.
3. Place the baking sheet in the oven. Bake the potato for about 40 minutes until cooked through. The cooking time will depend on how big the potato is.
4. Take the baking sheet out of the oven, then transfer the baked potato to a plate.
5. Use a knife to slice a hole in the middle of the potato lengthwise.
6. Sprinkle nutritional yeast into the hole, then top with black beans, avocado, and

salsa.

7. Sprinkle cilantro, salt, and pepper all over the potato.
8. Serve while hot with lime wedges on the side.

Light and Crispy Tofu

To make tofu that is perfectly crispy and light, you must squeeze out any excess moisture. This simple dish is easy to make and you can use the tofu in different dishes.

Time	25 minutes
Serving Size	3 servings
Prep Time	15 minutes
Cook Time	10 minutes

Nutritional Facts:
Calories: 187 kcal
Carbs: 13.5 grams
Fat: 12.3 grams
Protein: 7.9 grams

Ingredients:

- ½ tsp sriracha
- 1 tsp garlic salt
- 1 tsp onion powder
- 2 tsp agave syrup
- 1 tbsp cornstarch
- 2 tbsp soy sauce (preferably low-sodium)
- 2 tbsp white sesame seeds
- 3 tbsp lime juice (freshly squeezed)
- 3 tbsp olive oil
- ½ cup of breadcrumbs
- 1 block of tofu (firm, drained)
- 2 scallions (green parts sliced thinly, white parts minced)
- Black pepper
- Kosher salt

Directions:

1. Place the tofu in a clean kitchen towel, then wrap it up.
2. Place the wrapped tofu on a wire rack placed on a baking sheet.
3. Place a heavy object on top of the block of tofu for about 5 minutes to drain any excess moisture.
4. After pressing, unwrap the block of tofu.
5. Use a knife to cut the tofu in half, then cut each half into strips.
6. In a bowl, add the white parts of the

scallions, sriracha, agave syrup, lime juice, and soy sauce. Mix well and set aside.

7. In a shallow dish, add the cornstarch, breadcrumbs, onion powder, garlic salt, kosher salt, and pepper. Mix well.

8. Coat the tofu strips with the breading mixture. Make sure that each tofu strip is completely and evenly coated.

9. In a skillet, add olive oil over medium-high heat.

10. Once the oil is hot enough, add the tofu. Cook for about 4 to 5 minutes until golden brown.

11. Flip the tofu strips over. Cook for about 4 to 5 minutes until golden brown. If needed, cook the tofu in batches.

12. Place the cooked tofu on a plate lined with a paper towel.

13. Turn the heat down to low.

14. Add the sauce to the skillet. Cook for about 1 to 2 minutes until the sauce thickens.

15. Pour the sauce over the tofu, then sprinkle with the sliced scallion greens.

16. Serve while hot.

Crunchy Vegan Wraps

These plant-based wraps are crunchy, filling, and absolutely amazing. Prepare the lentils a day before to save time when making this dish.

Time	40 minutes
Serving Size	4 servings
Prep Time	20 minutes
Cook Time	20 minutes

Nutritional Facts:
Calories: 315 kcal
Carbs: 47 grams
Fat: 9.8 grams
Protein: 10.1 grams

Ingredients for the filling:

- ¼ tsp coriander (ground)
- ½ tsp cumin (ground)
- ½ tbsp extra-virgin olive oil
- 1 ½ tbsp tomato paste
- ⅛ cup of water (cold)
- 1 ¼ cups of green lentils (cooked)
- ½ small yellow onion (finely chopped)
- 1 clove of garlic (minced)
- 1 small chipotle pepper in adobo sauce
- Kosher salt

Ingredients for the wraps:

- ¼ cup of cherry tomatoes (cut in quarters)
- ½ cup of lettuce (shredded)
- ½ cup of vegan cheese (shredded)
- 4 large flour tortillas
- 4 tostada shells
- Vegetable oil (for cooking)
- Guacamole (for serving)

Directions:

1. In a skillet, add olive oil over medium heat.
2. Once the heat is hot enough, add the onion. Cook for about 6 minutes.
3. Add the garlic and continue cooking for 1

more minute.

4. Add the chipotle pepper and tomato paste. Cook for about 2 minutes while mashing the pepper.

5. Add the coriander, cumin, and salt. Mix well.

6. Add the lentils and water. Mix well and cook for about 5 minutes. If needed, add more water while cooking.

7. Take the skillet off the heat.

8. Place one flour tortilla on a plate.

9. Add some filling to the middle of the tortilla.

10. Top with a tostada shell, lettuce leaves, cherry tomatoes, and vegan cheese.

11. Take the bottom of the tortilla and fold it to the middle. Take the sides and fold them to the middle too.

12. Roll the tortilla tightly.

13. Repeat the assembling steps for the remaining vegan wraps.

14. In a skillet, add oil over medium heat.

15. Once the oil is hot enough, add the vegan wraps. Cook each side for about 3 minutes.

16. Transfer the vegan wraps to a plate.

17. Serve while hot with guacamole on the side.

Crispy Eggplant Parmesan

This crispy, gluten-free dish is incredibly tasty and comforting. The great thing about this dish is that you can use other veggies as the main ingredient too.

Time	45 minutes
Serving Size	2 servings
Prep Time	15 minutes
Cook Time	30 minutes

Nutritional Facts:
Calories: 334 kcal
Carbs: 40 grams
Fat: 18 grams
Protein: 4.7 grams

Ingredients for the coating:

- ½ tsp cornstarch
- ½ tsp oregano (dried)
- 1 tbsp arrowroot starch
- ⅛ cup of cornmeal
- ⅛ cup of vegan Parmesan cheese
- ¼ cup of almond milk (plain, unsweetened)
- ¼ cup of breadcrumbs (gluten-free)
- ¼ cup of flour (gluten-free)
- Sea salt

Ingredients for the eggplant:

- 2 tbsp avocado oil
- ½ cup of marinara sauce (homemade or store-bought)
- 1 narrow eggplant (sliced)

Directions:

1. Preheat your oven to 400°F. Use parchment paper to line a baking dish.

2. In a bowl, add the arrowroot starch, flour, and salt. Mix well.

3. In a second bowl, add the cornstarch and almond milk. Mix well.

4. In a third bowl, add the cornmeal, breadcrumbs, oregano, vegan Parmesan

cheese, and salt. Mix well.

5. Dip an eggplant slice in the flour mixture, then dip it in the almond milk mixture.

6. Finally, coat the eggplant slice in the breadcrumb mixture, then place on a plate.

7. Repeat the coating steps for the remaining eggplant slices.

8. In a skillet, add avocado oil over medium heat.

9. Once the oil is hot enough, add the eggplant slices.

10. Cook each side for about 2 to 3 minutes until golden brown. If needed, cook the eggplant slices in batches.

11. Place the cooked eggplant slices on the baking sheet.

12. Place the baking sheet in the oven. Bake the eggplant slices for about 10 to 15 minutes. Halfway through the cooking time, flip the eggplant slices over.

13. After baking, take the baking sheet out of the oven.

14. Serve the eggplant parmesan while hot with marinara sauce for dipping.

Meatless Pulled Pork Mini—Burgers

Just because you're going plant-based, it doesn't mean that you can't have fun dishes like a pulled pork sandwich. This recipe is meatless but super flavorful.

Time	1 hour, 25 minutes
Serving Size	3 servings
Prep Time	15 minutes
Cook Time	1 hour, 10 minutes

Nutritional Facts:
Calories: 697 kcal
Carbs: 86.2 grams
Fat: 20.8 grams
Protein: 59.7 grams

Ingredients for the sandwiches:

- ¼ tsp garlic powder
- ⅓ tsp smoked paprika
- ½ tbsp brown sugar
- ½ tbsp molasses
- 1 tbsp soy sauce
- 3 tbsp vegetable oil
- 1 ¼ cups of portobello mushrooms (cleaned, thinly sliced)
- 6 mini vegan slider buns
- Black pepper
- Kosher salt
- Toppings of your choice like hot sauce, lettuce, or pickle slices

Ingredients for the coleslaw:

- ¼ tsp celery seed
- ½ tsp apple cider vinegar
- ⅛ cup of vegan mayonnaise
- ¼ cup of carrots (grated)
- ½ cup of green cabbage (thinly sliced)
- A pinch of sugar
- Black pepper
- Kosher salt

Directions:

1. In a bowl, add the carrots and cabbage. Toss well.

2. In another bowl, add the vinegar, celery seed, mayonnaise, salt, pepper, and sugar. Mix well.

3. Drizzle the dressing over the veggies, then toss to coat.

4. Place the coleslaw in the refrigerator to chill until ready to serve.

5. Preheat your oven to 300°F. Use parchment paper to line a baking sheet, then brush some vegetable oil over the parchment paper. Use paper towels to line a second baking sheet.

6. On the baking sheet with parchment paper, add the sliced mushrooms. Arrange them in one layer and brush with the rest of the vegetable oil.

7. Place the baking sheet in the oven. Bake the mushrooms for about 25 to 30 minutes.

8. Take the baking sheet out of the oven. Flip the mushroom slices over, then continue baking for about 30 to 35 minutes until crispy and well-browned.

9. Take the baking sheet out of the oven. Place the mushroom slices on the baking sheet lined with paper towels to drain excess heat.

10. In a bowl, add the brown sugar, molasses, paprika, garlic powder, and soy

sauce. Mix well.

11. Add the mushroom slices to the bowl. Toss well to coat.

12. Place the marinated mushrooms back on the oiled baking sheet. Arrange them in one layer, then season with salt and pepper.

13. Place the baking sheet in the oven. Bake the mushrooms for about 5 minutes until crispy.

14. Take the baking sheet out of the oven. Take the bowl with coleslaw out of the refrigerator.

15. Add the "pulled pork" mushrooms to the bottom slices of the mini slider buns.

16. Top each bun with coleslaw and your choice of toppings, then add the top bun.

17. Serve while hot.

Veggie Ramen

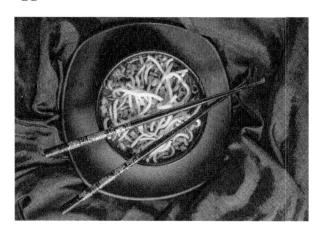

Ramen is a very popular dish all over the world. It can be made in different ways. Naturally, you will be making a purely plant-based version to comfort and fill you up.

Time	55 minutes
Serving Size	2 servings
Prep Time	20 minutes
Cook Time	35 minutes

Nutritional Facts:
Calories: 370 kcal
Carbs: 47.2 grams
Fat: 16.4 grams
Protein: 23.8 grams

Ingredients for the ramen:

- ½ tbsp sesame seeds (toasted)
- 1 tbsp vegetable oil
- 2 tbsp ginger (fresh, sliced)
- ⅛ cup of mirin
- ⅛ cup of shiitake mushrooms (dried)
- ⅛ cup of soy sauce
- ¼ cup of shiitake mushrooms (fresh, stems removed, caps reserved)
- 2 cups of vegetable stock (homemade or store-bought)
- 1 pack of ramen wheat noodles (cooked)
- 1 carrot (peeled, sliced)
- 1 head of baby bok choy (cut into quarters)
- 1 small yellow onion (chopped)
- 2 small pieces of kombu
- 3 green onions (chopped)
- 5 cloves of garlic (smashed)
- Kosher salt
- Toppings like sesame seeds, sesame oil, and green onions

Ingredients for the veggies:

- 1 tsp ginger (fresh, grated)
- ½ tbsp red miso paste
- ½ tbsp vegetable oil
- ¼ cup of edamame (shelled)
- ⅓ cup of baby portobello mushrooms

(stems removed, cut into quarters)

- ⅓ cup of shiitake mushrooms (the reserved caps)
- 1 carrot (peeled, thinly sliced)
- 1 clove of garlic (grated)
- 1 green onion (white parts minced, green parts thinly sliced)
- 1 head of baby bok choy (cut into quarters)
- Kosher salt

Directions:

1. In a Dutch oven, add vegetable oil over high heat.
2. Once the oil is hot enough, add the garlic, carrot, ginger, onion, and salt. Cook for about 7 minutes while stirring occasionally.
3. Add the kombu, shiitake mushroom stems, dried shiitake mushrooms, green onions, and bok choy. Mix well.
4. Add the vegetable stock and stir well. Bring the mixture to a boil.
5. Once boiling, turn the heat down to medium. Cover the Dutch oven with a lid and cook the broth for about 25 minutes.
6. While cooking the broth, prepare the veggies. Preheat your oven to 425°F. Use aluminum foil to line a baking sheet.

7. In a bowl, add the green onion, miso paste, ginger, garlic, and ⅔ of the vegetable oil. Mix well.

8. Add the carrots and toss to coat. Place the carrots on one side of the baking sheet.

9. Add the baby portobello mushrooms and the shiitake mushrooms, then toss to coat. Place on the other side of the baking sheet.

10. Place the baking sheet in the oven. Roast the veggies for about 5 minutes.

11. In a bowl, add the edamame, bok choy, salt, and the rest of the vegetable oil. Toss well to coat.

12. Take the baking sheet out of the oven. Make space in the middle by moving the veggies to the side. Add the edamame and bok choy.

13. Place the baking sheet back in the oven. Roast the vegetables for about 15 minutes until golden and tender.

14. After simmering the broth, pour the mixture through a fine-mesh strainer. Collect the broth in a bowl. Drain all of the liquid by using a spoon to mash the veggies.

15. Pour the broth back into the Dutch oven.

16. In a bowl, add the soy sauce and mirin. Mix well.

17. Prepare two bowls and divide the cooked ramen noodles between the bowls.
18. Pour half of the broth into one bowl and the rest into the other bowl.
19. Take the baking sheet out of the oven and divide the roasted veggies between the two ramen bowls.
20. Drizzle with the mirin-soy sauce mixture, then top with your choice of toppings.
21. Serve immediately.

CHAPTER 6
SUPER EASY SMOOTHIES AND OTHER DRINKS

Did you know that you can also make plant-based smoothies and other refreshing drinks right in your kitchen? You don't have to go to restaurants to sip on healthy and tasty beverages. As for smoothies, the great thing about them is that you can even have them as a snack or a light meal. In this chapter, you will learn how to make super simple smoothies and drinks.

Birthday Smoothie

This delicious smoothie is packed with protein and yet, it tastes like batter you would use to bake a cake. Imagine that! Try this smoothie for something fun and healthy.

Time	5 minutes
Serving Size	1 serving
Prep Time	5 minutes
Cook Time	no cooking time

Nutritional Facts:
Calories: 266 kcal
Carbs: 43 grams
Fat: 5 grams
Protein: 13 grams

Ingredients:

- 1 tsp vanilla extract
- ¼ cup of rolled oats
- 1 cup of cashew milk
- 1 scoop of protein powder (vegan, vanilla flavored)
- 1 banana (frozen, peeled, sliced)
- 1 tbsp sprinkles (for serving)
- Coconut whipped cream (for serving)

Directions:

1. In a blender, add all of the ingredients.
2. Blend everything together until you get a smooth and creamy texture.
3. Pour the smoothie into a glass.
4. Top with whipped cream and sprinkles.
5. Serve immediately.

Blueberry Latte Smoothie

This recipe isn't just for a simple smoothie. It's a combination of chia pudding and a smoothie. It's filling, delicious, and packed with nutritious plant goodness.

Time	10 minutes (chilling time not included)
Serving Size	2 servings
Prep Time	10 minutes
Cook Time	no cooking time

Nutritional Facts:
Calories: 291 kcal
Carbs: 38 grams
Fat: 14 grams
Protein: 7 grams

Ingredients for the chia pudding:

- 1 tbsp maple syrup
- ¼ cup of chia seeds
- ½ cup of almond milk (you can also use coconut milk)
- ½ cup of cold brew coffee (you can also use brewed coffee that has been cooled)

Ingredients for the smoothie:

- 1 tsp vanilla extract

- 1 cup of cashew yogurt (you can also use other types of non-dairy yogurt)
- 1 ½ cups of blueberries (frozen)

Directions:

1. In a blender, add all of the ingredients for the chia pudding.
2. Blend until everything is well-combined.
3. Pour the pudding into a jar with a lid. Place the jar in the refrigerator and chill for about 8 hours.
4. After chilling, take the jar of chia pudding out of the refrigerator.
5. In a blender, add all of the ingredients for the smoothie.
6. Blend until you get a creamy and smooth mixture.
7. Prepare two glasses and divide the smoothie between them.
8. Top each smoothie with chia pudding.
9. Serve immediately.

Milky Golden Smoothie

Golden milk is a traditional beverage from India. It's simple, healthy, and delicious. For this recipe, you will be transforming this beverage into a refreshing smoothie.

Time	5 minutes
Serving Size	1 serving
Prep Time	5 minutes
Cook Time	no cooking time

Nutritional Facts:
Calories: 295 kcal
Carbs: 43.7 grams
Fat: 13.9 grams
Protein: 3.5 grams

Ingredients:
- ¼ tsp black pepper
- ¼ tsp cardamom (ground)
- ¼ tsp cinnamon (ground)
- ¼ tsp clove (ground)
- ¼ tsp nutmeg (ground)
- ½ tsp turmeric (ground)
- 1 tbsp ginger (fresh)
- ¼ cup of carrot juice (fresh, homemade or store-bought)
- 1 cup of banana (sliced, peeled, frozen)

- 1 cup of light coconut milk (light, you can also use almond milk)
- 1 tbsp hemp seeds (for serving)

Directions:

1. In a blender, add the coconut milk, banana, nutmeg, cinnamon, ginger, turmeric, and pepper.
2. Blend until you get a creamy and smooth texture.
3. Add the clove, carrot juice, and cardamom, then continue blending until smooth. If the mixture is too thick, add more coconut milk. If the mixture is too thin, add more frozen banana slices.
4. Pour the smoothie into a glass.
5. Top with hemp seeds and serve immediately.

Choco—Mango Smoothie

This creamy smoothie combines the sweetness of chocolate with the refreshing flavor of mango. It doesn't require any sugar and it's super fun to drink!

Time	5 minutes
Serving Size	2 servings
Prep Time	5 minutes
Cook Time	no cooking time

Nutritional Facts:
Calories: 348 kcal
Carbs: 81 grams
Fat: 3 grams
Protein: 5 grams

Ingredients:

- 1 tsp vanilla extract
- 1 tsp ginger (fresh, grated)
- 1 tsp turmeric powder
- 2 tbsp cocoa
- 1 cup of almond yogurt
- ½ sweet potato (cooked)
- 2 mangoes (frozen, pcclcd, cut into cubes)
- A pinch of black pepper
- Toppings like cacao nibs and crushed

almonds

Directions:

1. In a blender, add the sweet potato, mangoes, almond yogurt, turmeric, ginger, vanilla extract, and black pepper.
2. Blend until you get a creamy and smooth mixture. If the mixture is too thick, add some water to it.
3. Prepare two glasses. Fill each glass halfway with the smoothie.
4. Add the cocoa to the blender. Blend until the cocoa is fully incorporated.
5. Pour the chocolatey smoothie into the two glasses.
6. Use a long spoon to swirl the smoothie halves in each glass.
7. Sprinkle your choice of toppings into each glass and serve immediately.

Sweet Veggie Smoothie

After indulging in a chocolatey smoothie, let's try something healthier. For this recipe, you will combine fruits and veggies to make a sweet and nutritious treat.

Time	5 minutes
Serving Size	2 servings
Prep Time	5 minutes
Cook Time	no cooking time

Nutritional Facts:
Calories: 367 kcal
Carbs: 28.2 grams
Fat: 14.6 grams
Protein: 34.4 grams

Ingredients:
- 2 tbsp chia seeds
- 2 tbsp flaxseed (ground)
- ½ cup of protein powder (vegan, vanilla)
- 3 cups of baby spinach
- 3 cups of mixed berries (frozen)
- 4 cups of almond milk (unsweetened)

Directions:
1. In a blender, add all of the ingredients.

2. Blend until creamy and smooth.
3. Prepare two glasses and divide the smoothie between them.
4. Serve immediately.

PLANT-BASED DIET FOR BEGINNERS

Comforting Hot Chocolate

There is nothing more comforting than a steaming cup of hot chocolate to warm you up when it's chilly. Here's a vegan-friendly twist on the classic drink.

Time	5 minutes
Serving Size	2 servings
Prep Time	5 minutes
Cook Time	no cooking time

Nutritional Facts:
Calories: 642 kcal
Carbs: 36.4 grams
Fat: 58 grams
Protein: 6.5 grams

Ingredients:

- 2 tbsp cocoa powder
- 3 tbsp maple syrup
- 2 cups of oat milk (you can also use other types of vegan milk like almond or cashew)

Dircctions:

1. In a blender, add all of the ingredients.
2. Blend until smooth and creamy.
3. Prepare two glasses and pour the

smoothie into each of them.
4. Serve immediately.

Trendy Dalgona Coffee

Dalgona coffee is a popular and trendy drink inspired by the Dalgona candy from South Korea. Here's a recipe for the dairy-free version to include in your plant-based diet.

Time	10 minutes
Serving Size	2 servings
Prep Time	10 minutes
Cook Time	no cooking time

Nutritional Facts:
Calories: 81.6 kcal
Carbs: 16.3 grams
Fat: 1.5 grams
Protein: 1.2 grams

Ingredients:

- 2 tbsp instant coffee
- 2 tbsp sugar
- 2 tbsp water (hot)
- 1 cup of almond milk
- 1 cup of ice cubes
- A pinch of cinnamon (ground, for serving)
- A pinch of sugar (for serving)

Directions:

1. In a bowl, add the instant coffee and sugar. Mix well.
2. Add the hot water and use a spoon to dissolve the coffee and sugar.
3. Whisk the mixture for a few minutes until stiff peaks start to form. The texture should be light and velvety.
4. Prepare two glasses and add ½ cup of ice cubes to each.
5. Fill each glass with ½ cup of almond milk.
6. Use a spoon to top each glass with the coffee whip.
7. Top with sugar and cinnamon.
8. Serve immediately.

Refreshing Pink Drink

This pink drink looks pretty and tastes amazing. It's a refreshing beverage with wonderfully fresh and fruity flavors for you to enjoy.

Time	25 minutes
Serving Size	2 servings
Prep Time	5 minutes
Cook Time	20 minutes

Nutritional Facts:
Calories: 55 kcal
Carbs: 9.4 grams
Fat: 2 grams
Protein: 0.8 grams

Ingredients:

- ½ tbsp maple syrup
- ¼ cup of coconut milk (light)
- ¼ cup of orange juice
- 1 cup of water
- 1 hibiscus tea bag
- 4 strawberries (ripe, hulled, thinly sliced)

Directions:

1. In a pot, add the water over medium heat. Bring to a boil.
2. Turn the heat down to low and allow to

simmer for about 5 minutes

3. Place the tea bag in a heat-proof pitcher, then pour the water into it.
4. Add the maple syrup and mix well.
5. Add half of the strawberries and mix well.
6. Let the mixture steep in the water for about 10 to 15 minutes.
7. After steeping, remove the tea bag and discard.
8. Pour the coconut milk and orange juice into the pitcher. Mix well to combine.
9. Prepare two glasses and divide the pink drink between them.
10. Top each glass with the rest of the sliced strawberries.
11. Serve immediately.

Fruity Spritzer

If you want something refreshing and light, this is a perfect choice. It's super easy to make and you can enjoy it at any time of the year!

Time	10 minutes (freezing time not included)
Serving Size	5 servings
Prep Time	10 minutes
Cook Time	no cooking time

Nutritional Facts:
Calories: 120 kcal
Carbs: 19 grams
Fat: 0 grams
Protein: 1 gram

Ingredients:

- 1 ½ cups of mango juice
- 1 ½ cups of orange juice
- 1 ½ cups of peach juice
- 2 cups of seltzer water
- ½ bottle of white wine
- Orange slices (for serving, you can also add peach and mango slices)

Directions:

1. Pour one of the juices into a big pitcher

or jar. Make sure the other ingredients will fit into the pitcher too.

2. Place the pitcher in the freezer. Allow the juice to harden without becoming completely frozen.

3. After freezing, take the pitcher out of the freezer.

4. Use a knife to gently break up the hardened juice into chunks.

5. Pour the seltzer water, white wine, and the rest of the juice into the pitcher. Stir until well combined.

6. Add the orange slices to the pitcher and serve.

Blackberry Cooler

This tasty frozen concoction is sweet, refreshing, and a little bit tart. If you want to make it fancy, line the rim of your glass with sugar before pouring the liquid into it.

Time	5 minutes
Serving Size	3 servings
Prep Time	5 minutes
Cook Time	no cooking time

Nutritional Facts:
Calories: 369 kcal
Carbs: 38.2 grams
Fat: 10.3 grams
Protein: 2.9 grams

Ingredients:

- 2 tbsp lime juice (freshly squeezed)
- ¼ cup of maple syrup
- ½ cup of coconut milk
- ¾ cup of rum
- 1 cup of ice
- 3 cups of blackberries (frozen)

Directions:

1. In a blender, add all of the ingredients.

2. Blend until you get a smooth and creamy texture.
3. Prepare three glasses and divide the blackberry cooler between them.
4. Serve immediately.

CHAPTER 7
SAUCES, DIPS, AND DRESSINGS

Make your salads and other dishes more flavorful by serving them with sauces, dips, and dressings. The wonderful thing about plant-based foods is that they are very flavorful. Breaking these foods down and combining them to make sauces, dips, and dressings will give you tasty results each time. In this chapter, you will learn how to make some versatile accompaniments to your plant-based meals.

Honey—Garlic Sauce

This recipe only requires five ingredients and a few minutes to put together. Use it as a marinade or as a dipping sauce for your favorite fried foods.

Time	10 minutes
Serving Size	¾ cup
Prep Time	5 minutes
Cook Time	5 minutes

Nutritional Facts:
Calories: 217 kcal
Carbs: 36 grams
Fat: 7.6 grams
Protein: 1.6 grams

Ingredients:

- 1 tsp dry mustard powder
- 2 tbsp vegan butter
- 3 tbsp soy sauce
- ½ cup of maple syrup
- 2 cloves of garlic (minced)

Directions:

1. In a saucepan, add vegan butter over medium-high heat.
2. Once the butter has melted, add the garlic. Sauté for about 1 to 2 minutes.
3. Add the mustard powder, maple syrup, and soy sauce. Mix well and cook for about 3 minutes.
4. Pour the sauce into a bowl.
5. Serve while warm or allow to cool down completely if you will use it as a marinade.

Creamy Hollandaise Sauce

Level up your breakfast dishes by drizzling some creamy homemade hollandaise sauce over them. This sauce recipe is very simple but super tasty.

Time	10 minutes
Serving Size	2 cups
Prep Time	7 minutes
Cook Time	3 minutes

Nutritional Facts:
Calories: 82 kcal
Carbs: 4.1 grams
Fat: 5.7 grams
Protein: 2 grams

Ingredients:

- ¼ tsp cayenne pepper
- ¼ tsp white pepper
- 1 tsp salt
- 3 tbsp lemon juice (freshly squeezed)
- 2 ½ tbsp vegan egg yolk powder
- ⅓ cup of vegan butter (melted)
- 1 ¼ cups of water (hot)

Directions:

1. In a food processor, add the egg yolk powder and hot water.
2. Blend until you get a smooth texture. If needed, add more hot water.
3. Add the lemon juice, then blend to combine.
4. Add the cayenne, salt, and pepper, then blend to combine.
5. In a saucepan, add vegan butter over medium-high heat.
6. Once the butter has melted, slowly pour it into the food processor while blending. Keep blending until all of the ingredients are well combined and form a smooth, creamy texture.
7. Pour the sauce into a bowl.
8. Allow to cool down slightly before serving.

Pimiento and Cheese Dip

This dip is so delicious and creamy that you will keep wanting to dip veggies and other foods into it. The ingredients come together perfectly to create an amazing dip!

Time	5 minutes (chilling time not included)
Serving Size	2 cups
Prep Time	5 minutes
Cook Time	no cooking time

Nutritional Facts:
Calories: 304 kcal
Carbs: 18.1 grams
Fat: 24 grams
Protein: 8.2 grams

Ingredients:

- ½ tsp salt
- ½ tsp smoked paprika
- 1 tsp sriracha
- 2 tsp Dijon mustard
- 2 tbsp pimento peppers (jarred)
- 3 tbsp lemon juice (freshly squeezed)
- ½ cup of water
- 1 ½ cups of cashews (raw)
- 1 clove of garlic
- Black pepper
- 1 tsp chives (fresh, chopped, for garnish)

Directions:

1. In a blender, add the water, cashews, Dijon mustard, pimento peppers, sriracha, lemon juice, smoked paprika, garlic, salt, and pepper.
2. Blend until you get a smooth and creamy texture. If the mixture is too thick, add more water into the blender. Keep adding water until you get the desired consistency.
3. Spoon the dip into a jar or an airtight container. Place the jar in the refrigerator to chill until ready to serve.
4. After chilling, take the jar out of the refrigerator.
5. Scoop some dip into a bowl, then top with

chopped chives.

6. Serve chilled with crackers, vegetable sticks, or any other food items.

Creamy French Onion Dip

This dip is tangy, creamy, and super savory. Enjoy dipping homemade chips and veggie sticks in it for an amazing snack or appetizer.

Time	10 minutes (chilling time not included)
Serving Size	4 servings
Prep Time	10 minutes
Cook Time	no cooking time

Nutritional Facts:
Calories: 176 kcal
Carbs: 10.7 grams
Fat: 12.4 grams
Protein: 5.4 grams

Ingredients for the cashew sour cream:

- ¾ tsp apple cider vinegar
- 1 tbsp lemon juice (freshly squeezed)
- ½ cup of water
- 1 cup of cashews (raw, soaked overnight)
- A pinch of mineral salt

Ingredients for the dip:

- ¼ tsp onion powder
- ½ tsp sea salt
- 2 tbsp chives (fresh, chopped)
- ½ cup of caramelized onions (packed, chopped, you can also make your own caramelized onions)
- 1 cup of cashew sour cream
- Black pepper
- Potato chips or veggie sticks (for serving)

Directions:

1. In a blender, add all of the cashew sour cream ingredients.
2. Blend until you get a creamy texture. If needed, as more water to get the consistency you desire.
3. Pour the sour cream into a jar with a lid. Place the jar in the refrigerator to chill for about 20 minutes.
4. After chilling, take the cashew sour

cream out of the refrigerator.

5. Add 1 cup of cashew sour cream to a bowl along with the caramelized onions, chives, onion powder, salt, and pepper. Mix well

6. Place the refrigerator in a bowl and chill for about 1 hour.

7. Serve chilled with potato chips or veggie sticks.

Spinach and Artichoke Dip

This veggie dip is creamy, comforting, and low in fat. Whip up a batch for yourself, then store it in the refrigerator or serve it the next time you host a party.

Time	30 minutes
Serving Size	4 servings
Prep Time	10 minutes
Cook Time	20 minutes

Nutritional Facts:
Calories: 413 kcal
Carbs: 75.9 grams
Fat: 1.2 grams
Protein: 28.7 grams

Ingredients:

- ½ tsp garlic powder
- ½ tsp onion powder
- ½ tsp salt
- 1 tsp lemon juice (freshly squeezed)
- 2 tbsp nutritional yeast
- ½ cup of artichoke hearts (jarred, drained)
- ½ cup of water
- 1 cup of spinach
- 1 ¾ cups of white beans (canned, drained, warmed)

Directions:

1. Preheat your oven to 350˚F.

2. In a blender, add the beans, water, garlic powder, onion powder, and salt. Blend until creamy and smooth.

3. Add the lemon juice and artichoke hearts. Continue blending until creamy and smooth.

4. Transfer the dip to an oven-safe container.

5. Tear the spinach into small pieces. Mix the pieces into the dip.

6. Place the oven-safe container in the oven. Bake the dip for about 20 minutes.

7. Take the oven-safe container out of the oven.

8. Allow the dip to cool down slightly before serving.

Thai—Style Peanut Dressing

Peanut dressing is very popular in Thailand. It's used for salads, meat dishes, fish, and more. After making this dressing, you can use it in different ways too!

Time	30 minutes
Serving Size	4 servings
Prep Time	15 minutes
Cook Time	15 minutes

Nutritional Facts:
Calories: 113 kcal
Carbs: 17.2 grams
Fat: 4.3 grams
Protein: 3.5 grams

Ingredients:

- 1 ½ tsp sambal oelek
- 1 ½ tsp soy sauce
- 1 tbsp basil (fresh, chopped)
- 2 tbsp lime juice (freshly squeezed)
- 2 tbsp maple syrup
- 2 tbsp peanut butter
- ¼ cup of water
- ½ cup of roasted red bell pepper (jarred, rinsed, drained)
- 1 eggplant (peeled, sliced)
- 2 cloves of garlic
- Black pepper
- Sea salt

Directions:

1. In a skillet, add the water and eggplant over medium heat.
2. Cover the skillet with a lid. Cook the eggplant for about 10 to 15 minutes while stirring occasionally. If needed, add more water to prevent the eggplant from sticking to the bottom of the pan.
3. Transfer the eggplant to a bowl and let it cool down for about 10 minutes.
4. After cooling, add the eggplant to a blender along with the rest of the ingredients, except for the basil.
5. Blend until you get a smooth and creamy

consistency.

6. Pour the mixture into a jar with a lid.
7. Add the basil and mix well.
8. Cover the jar and place it in the refrigerator.
9. Serve chilled.

Ranch Dressing

Ranch is another popular dressing that can be used in different ways. In this recipe, you need simple ingredients to create a plant-based dressing that tastes like the real thing.

Time	5 minutes
Serving Size	6 servings
Prep Time	5 minutes
Cook Time	no cooking time

Nutritional Facts:
Calories: 141 kcal
Carbs: 8.9 grams
Fat: 10.7 grams
Protein: 4.4 grams

Ingredients:

- ¼ tsp dill (dried)
- ½ tsp garlic powder
- ½ tsp onion powder
- ½ tsp sea salt
- 1 tbsp nutritional yeast
- 2 tbsp lemon juice
- ⅓ cup of cucumber (peeled, diced)
- ½ cup of water
- 1 cup of cashews (raw, soaked overnight)
- Chives (fresh, chopped, for garnish)

Directions:

1. In a blender, add the water, cashews, nutritional yeast, cucumber, lemon juice, dill, onion powder, garlic powder, and salt.
2. Blend until creamy and smooth.
3. Pour the dressing into a bowl.
4. Garnish with chives before serving.

Roasted Hummus

In itself, hummus already tastes wonderful. For this recipe, you will be using slow-roasted tomatoes to create a flavorful and creamy sauce to pair with anything!

Time	3 hours, 20 minutes
Serving Size	6 servings
Prep Time	20 minutes
Cook Time	3 hours

Nutritional Facts:
Calories: 812 kcal
Carbs: 93 grams
Fat: 38.4 grams
Protein: 32.5 grams

Ingredients for the slow-roasted tomatoes:

- ½ tsp pepper
- ½ tsp salt
- ½ tsp thyme (dried)
- ½ tbsp sugar
- 1 tbsp olive oil
- 4 cups of cherry tomatoes (cut in half, you can also use grape tomatoes)
- 1 clove of garlic (minced)

Ingredients for the hummus:

- ½ tsp pepper
- ½ tsp salt
- 1 ½ tbsp lemon juice (freshly squeezed)
- 2 tbsp olive oil
- 3 tbsp ice water
- ⅔ cup of slow-roasted tomatoes
- 1 cup of tahini paste
- 3 ½ cups of chickpeas (canned, drained, rinsed, peeled)
- 2 cloves of garlic
- Oregano (fresh, chopped, for garnish)
- Pita (homemade or store-bought, sliced into wedges, for serving)

Directions:

1. Preheat your oven to 300°F. Use

parchment paper to line a baking sheet.

2. In a bowl, add the garlic, cherry tomatoes, thyme, sugar, salt, and olive oil. Toss well to coat the tomatoes.

3. Place the tomatoes on the baking sheet. Arrange them in one layer.

4. Place the baking sheet in the oven. Roast the tomatoes for about 2 ½ to 3 hours. Every half an hour or so, toss the tomatoes around to cook them evenly.

5. Take the baking sheet out of the oven. Allow the tomatoes to cool down completely. Once cool, take ⅔ cup to add to the hummus and store the rest in an airtight container.

6. In a food processor, add chickpeas, lemon juice, garlic, tahini, salt, and pepper. Blend until you get a creamy and smooth texture.

7. Add the tomatoes and continue blending until well combined.

8. Drizzle the ice water into the food processor, then continue blending for about 1 to 2 minutes.

9. Scoop the hummus into a bowl and top with oregano.

10. Serve with pita wedges.

Vibrant Beetroot Hummus

For this hummus recipe, you will use beet as the main ingredient. It has a vibrant color and a wonderful flavor that pairs well with different foods.

Time	5 minutes
Serving Size	4 servings
Prep Time	5 minutes
Cook Time	no cooking time

Nutritional Facts:
Calories: 551 kcal
Carbs: 72.3 grams
Fat: 21.2 grams
Protein: 22.7 grams

Ingredients:

- 1 tsp cumin (ground)
- 1 tsp fine salt
- 1 tbsp lemon zest
- 2 tbsp tahini sauce
- 3 tbsp olive oil
- 3 ½ tbsp lemon juice (freshly squeezed)
- ¾ cup of beetroots (roasted or cooked, cut into cubes)
- 1 ¾ cup of chickpeas (canned, drained)
- 1 clove of garlic (minced)
- Black pepper

Directions:

1. In a food processor, add all of the ingredients.
2. Blend until you get a creamy and smooth texture. If needed, add some water or some of the liquid from the canned chickpeas.
3. Transfer the hummus to a bowl and serve.

Baba Ganoush

Eggplant is the main ingredient for this traditional Asian dip. It's savory, creamy, smoky, and pairs well with different types of food.

Time	1 hour, 10 minutes
Serving Size	4 servings
Prep Time	10 minutes
Cook Time	1 hour

Nutritional Facts:
Calories: 223 kcal
Carbs: 20 grams
Fat: 15.7 grams
Protein: 5.4 grams

Ingredients:

- ½ tsp sea salt
- 2 tbsp extra-virgin olive oil
- 3 tbsp lemon juice (freshly squeezed)
- ¼ cup of tahini
- 2 cloves of garlic
- 2 eggplants
- A pinch of red pepper flakes (for garnish)
- A pinch of smoked paprika (for garnish)
- Parsley (fresh, finely chopped, for garnish)
- Pita or veggie sticks (for serving)

Directions:

1. Preheat your oven to 400°F.
2. Chop the stems off the eggplants. Wrap each of them in aluminum foil and place them on a baking sheet.
3. Place the baking sheet in the oven. Roast the eggplants for about 55 minutes to 1 hour.
4. Take the baking sheet out of the oven. Allow the eggplants to cool down.
5. Once cool enough to handle, unwrap the eggplants and peel the skin off.
6. Remove large clumps of seeds, then place the flesh in a strainer for about 20 minutes to drain any excess moisture.
7. In a food processor, add the eggplants,

garlic, olive oil, lemon juice, tahini, and salt.

8. Blend until you get a smooth and creamy texture.

9. Transfer the mixture to a bowl. Top with red pepper flakes, smoked paprika, and parsley.

10. Serve with veggie sticks or pita wedges.

CHAPTER 8
INDULGENT DESSERT RECIPES

While following a plant-based diet, give in to your sweet tooth cravings by making sweet and healthy treats right in your kitchen. In this chapter, you will learn how to make some amazingly simple dishes that burst with flavor. Indulge in these desserts on your own or share them with your whole family!

Peanut Butter Cookie Bites

Experience happiness with each bite of this no-bake dessert. Making these cookie bites is so easy that this might become one of your favorite sweet treats.

Time	15 minutes (freezing time not included)
Serving Size	6 servings
Prep Time	10 minutes
Cook Time	5 minutes

Nutritional Facts:
Calories: 213 kcal
Carbs: 17.3 grams
Fat: 14.8 grams
Protein: 3.9 grams

Ingredients:

- 1 tsp vanilla extract
- 1 tbsp maple syrup
- 2 tbsp peanut butter
- 6 tbsp coconut oil
- ¼ cup of dark cocoa powder
- ¼ cup of maple syrup
- ¼ cup of peanut butter
- 1 cup of rolled oats
- A pinch of kosher salt

Directions:

1. Line a mini muffin tin with mini cupcake liners.
2. In a saucepan, add 3 tablespoons of coconut oil over low heat.
3. Once the oil is hot enough, add the cocoa powder, ¼ cup maple syrup, 2 tablespoons of peanut butter, vanilla extract, and kosher salt. Mix well.
4. Take the saucepan off the heat. Add the rolled oats and mix until well combined.
5. Spoon the mixture into the mini cupcake liners.
6. In a saucepan, add 1 tablespoon of maple syrup, 1 tablespoon of coconut oil, and ¼ cup of peanut butter over low heat. Mix well.
7. Top each peanut butter bite with the

peanut butter mixture.

8. Place the mini muffin tin in the refrigerator. Freeze for about 15 to 20 minutes.

9. Serve chilled and store any leftovers in the refrigerator.

Fudgy Chocolate Truffles

This nut-free dessert is perfectly fudgy and indulgent. You only need a few ingredients to make these truffles that you can enjoy at the end of every meal.

Time	30 minutes (free time not included)
Serving Size	5 servings
Prep Time	30 minutes
Cook Time	No cooking time

Nutritional Facts:
Calories: 103 kcal
Carbs: 20 grams
Fat: 3 grams
Protein: 2 grams

Ingredients:

- ½ tsp sea salt
- 1 tsp vanilla extract
- 6 tbsp cacao powder (raw)
- ¼ cup of oat flour
- ½ cup of dark chocolate (dairy-free, chopped)
- 1 small beet (cooked, peeled, chopped)
- 12 Medjool dates (pits removed)
- Optional coating ingredients like shredded coconut (unsweetened), cacao powder (raw), hemp seeds, beetroot powder, or chopped nuts

Directions:

1. In a food processor, add the dates, beet, 4 tablespoons of cacao powder, vanilla extract, and salt.
2. Blend until you get a sticky texture.
3. Add the oat flour and the rest of the cacao powder.
4. Blend until you form a sticky dough.
5. Place the dough in a bowl, then use cling wrap to cover the bowl.
6. Place the bowl in the freezer for about 1 to 2 hours.
7. After freezing, use parchment paper to line a baking sheet, then take the bowl out of the freezer.

8. In a microwave-safe bowl, add the dark chocolate.

9. Heat in the microwave in 30-second intervals and mix well until the chocolate melts completely.

10. Scoop portions of the sticky dough, then use your hands to roll each portion into a ball. Place the truffles on the baking sheet.

11. Dip each truffle into the melted chocolate, then place it back on the baking sheet. Coat the truffles with your choice of coating ingredients.

12. Place the baking sheet in the freezer to set for about 20 to 30 minutes.

13. Serve chilled and store any leftovers in an airtight container.

Pumpkin Pie Parfait

This parfait recipe is super easy to make. Although chilling the pumpkin pudding takes time, when that step is done, assembling the parfaits will be a breeze!

Time	15 minutes (chilling time not included)
Serving Size	4 servings
Prep Time	15 minutes
Cook Time	no cooking time

Nutritional Facts:
Calories: 329 kcal
Carbs: 24.4 grams
Fat: 25.7 grams
Protein: 5.1 grams

Ingredients:

- ¼ tsp sea salt
- 1 ½ tsp cinnamon
- 1 ½ tsp vanilla extract
- 2 tbsp almond butter (creamy)
- ¼ cup of maple syrup
- ½ cup of coconut solids (thick)
- ½ cup of pecans (toasted, crushed)
- 1 cup of pumpkin purée
- Coconut whip (for serving)

Directions:

1. In a blender, add all of the ingredients except for the coconut whip and pecans.
2. Pour the mixture into a bowl.
3. Place the bowl in the refrigerator to chill for about 4 to 6 hours. For a thicker pudding, chill overnight.
4. After chilling, take the bowl out of the refrigerator.
5. Prepare four parfait glasses. Layer each glass with pumpkin pudding and pecans.
6. Top with coconut whip and serve chilled.

Cookie Dough Dessert Bars

These dessert bars will satisfy your sweet tooth with every bite. You just need a couple of ingredients to make this dish and it doesn't even require cooking.

Time	15 minutes (chilling time not included)
Serving Size	4 servings
Prep Time	15 minutes
Cook Time	no cooking time

Nutritional Facts:
Calories: 179 kcal
Carbs: 28 grams
Fat: 7 grams
Protein: 3 grams

Ingredients:

- ½ tsp fine sea salt
- 2 tsp coconut oil (refined, melted)
- 1 tbsp vanilla extract
- 4 ½ tbsp maple syrup
- ¼ cup of tahini (you can also use cashew butter or almond butter)
- 1 cup of chocolate chips (vegan)
- 1 cup of Medjool dates (soft, pits removed)
- 2 ¾ cups of oat flour (preferably gluten-free)

Directions:

1. In a food processor, add the oat flour, maple syrup, dates, tahini, and vanilla extract. Blend until you form a sticky dough. If it's too dry, you may add some almond milk.
2. Transfer the dough to a bowl, then fold half of the chocolate chips into the dough.
3. Use parchment paper to line a baking sheet. The parchment paper should be longer than the baking sheet so that some excess hangs over the sides.
4. Add the dough to the baking sheet, then smoothen into a flat, even layer.
5. Place the baking sheet in the freezer. Freeze the mixture for about 30 minutes.

6. Just before taking the baking sheet out of the freezer, melt the chocolate chips.

7. In a microwave-safe bowl, add the coconut oil and the rest of the chocolate chips.

8. Place the bowl in the microwave and heat on high for about 30 seconds.

9. Take the bowl out and mix the ingredients together.

10. Repeat the heating and mixing steps in 30-second intervals until the chocolate chips have melted completely.

11. Take the baking sheet out of the freezer. Drizzle the melted chocolate all over the block of dessert bars.

12. Place the baking sheet back in the freezer for about 15 minutes for the chocolate to harden.

13. After freezing, take the baking sheet out of the freezer.

14. Slice into squares or rectangles before serving.

Nutty Frozen Yogurt

If you love frozen yogurt, you should try making it at home. This recipe gives you a delicious nutty flavor with an amazingly creamy texture.

Time	10 minutes (freezing time not included)
Serving Size	6 servings
Prep Time	10 minutes
Cook Time	no cooking time

Nutritional Facts:
Calories: 139 kcal
Carbs: 24.4 grams
Fat: 5.6 grams
Protein: 1.4 grams

Ingredients:

- ¼ tsp xanthan gum
- ¾ tsp almond extract
- 4 tbsp pistachios (raw, shelled, crushed)
- ¼ cup of maple syrup
- 1 cup of spinach
- 1 ½ cups of coconut yogurt (unsweetened)
- ½ avocado (peeled, sliced)
- 2 bananas (frozen, sliced)

Directions:

1. In a food processor, add the avocado, banana, yogurt, maple syrup, xanthan gum, almond extract, and half of the pistachios. Blend until thick and smooth.
2. Use parchment paper to line a loaf pan. Pour the mixture into the loaf pan.
3. Use a spatula to smoothen the surface, then top with the rest of the pistachios.
4. Place the loaf pan in the freezer for about 3 to 4 hours.
5. After freezing, take the loaf pan out of the freezer.
6. Scoop and serve!

Cheesecake Brownies

Combining the flavors of cheesecake and brownies makes for a sweet and tangy dessert. This decadent dish will surely impress your whole family from the first bite.

Time	1 hour
Serving Size	6 servings
Prep Time	20 minutes
Cook Time	40 minutes

Nutritional Facts:
Calories: 611 kcal
Carbs: 66.3 grams
Fat: 39.4 grams
Protein: 14.1 grams

Ingredients for the brownies:

- ½ tsp salt
- ¾ tsp baking powder
- 1 tbsp vanilla extract
- ½ cup of almond butter (smooth, unsalted, unsweetened, you can also use peanut butter)
- ⅔ cup of cocoa powder
- 1 cup of almond milk (unsweetened)
- 1 cup of flour (preferably gluten-free)
- 1 ¼ cups of cane sugar (organic)
- 3 flax eggs (combine 3 tbsp flaxseed meal and 6 tbsp water)

Ingredients for the cheesecake:

- ½ tsp lemon zest
- ½ tbsp lemon juice (freshly squeezed)
- ½ tbsp vanilla extract
- 1 tbsp cornstarch
- 2 tbsp cane sugar (organic)
- ¼ cup of cane sugar (organic)
- 1 cup of vegan cream cheese

Directions:

1. Preheat your oven to 350°F. Use parchment paper to line a metal pan.
2. Prepare the flax eggs, then allow to thicken for about 10 minutes.

3. After allowing the flax eggs to thicken, add them to a bowl along with the almond milk, cane sugar, vanilla extract, and almond butter. Mix until well combined.

4. Add the baking powder, cocoa powder, flour, and salt. Mix until well combined.

5. Set aside ¼ cup of brownie batter.

6. Pour the rest of the batter into the metal pan and smoothen the batter into an even layer. Set aside.

7. In a separate bowl, add ¼ cup of cane sugar and the vegan cream cheese.

8. Use a hand mixer to whisk the ingredients until you get a smooth texture.

9. Pour the cream cheese batter over the layer of brownie batter in the metal pan.

10. Smoothen the batter into an even layer.

11. Drizzle the reserved brownie batter over the cheesecake layer, then use a toothpick to swirl the mixture around creating a lovely pattern.

12. Place the metal pan in the oven. Bake the cheesecake brownies for about 35 to 40 minutes.

13. After baking, take the metal pan out of the oven. Allow the cheesecake brownies to cool down completely.

14. Slice and serve.

Deluxe Banana Split

Banana split is a classic dessert but for this recipe, you will make it more modern by adding salted caramel to the mix. It's amazingly delicious and decadent.

Time	15 minutes
Serving Size	2 servings
Prep Time	10 minutes
Cook Time	5 minutes

Nutritional Facts:
Calories: 932 kcal
Carbs: 136 grams
Fat: 40 grams
Protein: 17 grams

Ingredients:

- 2 tbsp brown sugar
- 2 tbsp maple syrup
- ¹/₁ cup of caramel sauce
- ¼ cup of peanuts (roasted)
- ⅓ cup of dark chocolate (melted)
- 2 bananas (sliced lengthwise without peeling)
- Salted caramel ice cream (vegan)
- Sea salt (for serving)

Directions:

1. Preheat your oven to 400°F.
2. Place the bananas on a baking tray with the sliced side facing up.
3. Sprinkle each banana with brown sugar.
4. Place the baking tray in the oven. Bake the bananas for about 3 to 5 minutes until caramelized.
5. Take the baking tray out of the oven. Allow the bananas to cool down.
6. In a pan, add the peanuts over medium heat. Toast them for about 1 minute.
7. Add the maple syrup, then sauté for about 2 to 3 minutes until the peanuts are fully coated and sticky.
8. Sprinkle some sea salt over the peanuts, then take the pan off the heat. Set aside.
9. Prepare two plates and add one banana

to each of them.

10. Top each banana with 2 or 3 scoops of salted caramel ice cream.

11. Drizzle melted chocolate and caramel sauce over the ice cream.

12. Top each banana split with caramelized peanuts and sea salt.

13. Serve immediately.

Strawberry Crumble

This is an easy summer dessert that's fruity, nutty, and has just the right amount of kick from the balsamic vinegar. You can even use blueberries for this recipe.

Time	30 minutes
Serving Size	4 servings
Prep Time	15 minutes
Cook Time	15 minutes

Nutritional Facts:
Calories: 195 kcal
Carbs: 28,9 grams
Fat: 8.8 grams
Protein: 3.3 grams

Ingredients:

- ⅛ tsp sea salt
- ½ tsp balsamic vinegar
- ½ tsp cinnamon
- 1 tbsp coconut oil (hardened)
- 1 tbsp water
- ¼ cup of almond flour
- ¼ cup coconut sugar
- ⅓ cup of pistachios (shelled, chopped)
- ⅓ cup of whole rolled oats
- 2 ½ cups of strawberries (chopped)
- Cooking spray
- Ice cream (vegan, vanilla or any other flavor, for serving)

Directions:

1. Preheat your oven to 350°F. Use cooking spray to lightly grease four ramekins.
2. In a food processor, add the flour, oats, coconut sugar, cinnamon, pistachios, and salt. Blend until just combined.
3. Add the coconut oil and blend for a few seconds.
4. Add the water and blend for a few seconds. The final mixture should have a crumbly texture.
5. In a bowl, add the balsamic vinegar and strawberries. Mix well.
6. Divide the strawberries between the four

ramekins, then top with the crumble mixture.

7. Place the ramekins in the oven. Bake the strawberry crumble for about 15 minutes.

8. Take the ramekins out of the oven. Allow the strawberry crumble to cool down for about 10 minutes.

9. Serve on its own or with a scoop of your favorite ice cream.

Banana Pudding

This delicious pudding is healthy and dairy-free. It's another easy recipe that comes together in a matter of minutes. It's so tasty that it might become one of your favorites!

Time	5 minutes
Serving Size	2 servings
Prep Time	5 minutes
Cook Time	no cooking time

Nutritional Facts:
Calories: 211 kcal
Carbs: 37 grams
Fat: 7 grams
Protein: 8 grams

Ingredients:

- 2 tbsp cocoa powder (unsweetened)
- ¼ cup of peanut butter (powdered)
- ¼ cup of water
- 2 bananas (peeled)
- 2 tbsp coconut (shredded, for garnish)

Directions:

1. In a bowl, add the bananas.
2. Use a fork or potato masher to mash the bananas.
3. Add the peanut butter, cocoa powder, and water. Stir well.
4. Prepare two bowls and divide the pudding between them.
5. Top with shredded coconut and serve.

Tropical Shaved Ice

Shaved ice is a very popular treat in Hawaii. The great thing about this refreshing treat is that you can make it in your kitchen using just a couple of fresh ingredients.

Time	20 minutes (freezing time not included)
Serving Size	4 servings
Prep Time	10 minutes
Cook Time	10 minutes

Nutritional Facts:
Calories: 398 kcal
Carbs: 91 grams
Fat: 6 grams
Protein: 2 grams

Ingredients:

- 1 cup of sugar (preferably superfine)
- 3 cups of water
- 1 ½ cups of mango juice
- 4 cups of strawberries (diced)
- ½ cup of coconut (toasted, for serving)
- 1 mango (peeled, diced, for serving)

Directions:

1. In a pot, add 1 cup of water and ¾ cup of sugar over medium heat. Bring to a boil.

2. Once boiling, take the pot off the heat. Add the rest of the water and mix well.

3. Pour the sweetened water into a baking dish. Place the baking dish in the freezer for about 5 hours. Every 30 minutes or so, stir the sweetened water to form ice crystals.

4. After freezing, prepare the rest of the ingredients. Pour the mango juice into a container with a spout for pouring.

5. In a blender, add the strawberries and the rest of the sugar. Blend until smooth.

6. Pour the mixture into a container with a spout for pouring.

7. Take the baking dish out of the oven and prepare four glasses. Divide the shaved ice into the glasses.

8. Pour the strawberry mixture and mango

juice into each of the glasses.

9. Top each glass with mango bits and toasted coconut.

10. Serve immediately.

CONCLUSION
COOKING FOR YOUR HEALTH

Cooking your own meals at home can be a lot of fun. In the process, you will learn more about plant-based foods and various cooking techniques. You will even learn more about yourself with each dish that you make.

Throughout this book, you have gained a wealth of knowledge about plant-based foods.

We started by defining what plant-based diets are and the benefits of following them. You also discovered some easy and practical beginner tips to help you get started. In the next chapter, you learned all about meal planning, a process that makes it much easier to start and stick with plant-based diets. In the same chapter, you also found out which foods to eat and avoid when you go plant-based. With all this information, you can start stocking up your kitchen with plant foods to use in your cooking.

And in the next six chapters, you learn tons of recipes to kick-start your plant-based journey. There were recipes for breakfast dishes; soups, salads, and appetizers; main course recipes you can have for lunch or dinner; smoothies and other refreshing drinks; sauces, dips, and dressings; and indulgent desserts to satisfy your sweet tooth cravings.

As promised at the beginning of this book, you now have everything you need to start transitioning into a plant-based diet. Going plant-based is one of the best things you can do for your health. By cooking your own food, you can focus on fresh, nutrient-dense ingredients instead of eating too many processed or packaged plant foods.

Remember that going plant-based can only be beneficial if you nourish your body with natural, whole foods. With all of the recipes here, you will be introduced to a wide range of dishes that use different types of ingredients. Start cooking now and discover how incredible a plant-based diet can be. Good luck!

FREE BONUS

https://www.subscribepage.com/hba_copy

REFERENCES

Images courtesy of -
https://unsplash.com/license

APA Abraham, L. (2021, August 23). *These vegan "crunchy wraps" taste even better than Taco Bell.* Delish. https://www.delish.com/cooking/recipe-ideas/a37051780/vegan-crunchwraps-recipe/

Alena. (2020, October 9). *Anti-inflammatory vegan lentil carrot soup (One-pot).* Nutriciously. https://nutriciously.com/vegan-lentil-soup/

Alena. (2021, May 19). *Chocolate mango smoothie.* Nutriciously. https://nutriciously.com/mango-chocolate-smoothie/

Alexander, H. (2019, November). *5 benefits of a plant-based diet.* MD Anderson Cancer Center. https://www.mdanderson.org/publications/focused-on-health/5-benefits-of-a-plant-based-diet.h20-1592991.html

Anthea. (2022, March 29). *Basil alfredo pasta (vegan).* Rainbow Nourishments. https://www.rainbownourishments.com/ba

sil-alfredo-zoodles

Beelman, M. M. (2020, January 27). *Easy vegan potato soup recipe*. Namely Marly. https://namelymarly.com/vegan-potato-soup/

Beelman, M. M. (2021, December 6). *Vegan tomato soup recipe*. Namely Marly. https://namelymarly.com/vegan-tomato-soup/

Benisek, A. (2021, September 30). *Plant-based diet tips for beginners*. WebMD. https://www.webmd.com/diet/plant-based-diet

Bernard, L. (2020, June 11). *Vegan breakfast skillet recipe (Dairy free/egg free/meatless)*. Make It Dairy Free. https://makeitdairyfree.com/dairy-free-breakfast-skillet-recipe/

Bodrug, C. (2020, October 20). *Fall vegan drinks*. PlantYou. https://plantyou.com/fall-vegan-drinks/

Bodrug, C. (2021, March 2). *10 best vegan smoothie recipes*. PlantYou. https://plantyou.com/10-best-vegan-smoothie-recipes/

Breyer, M. (n.d.). *10 Plant-based staples to stock a vegan kitchen*. Treehugger. https://www.treehugger.com/plant-based-staples-stock-vegan-kitchen-4856855

Briones, J. (2020, January 23). *Vegan cheesecake brownies (Gluten-free).* Sweet Simple Vegan. https://sweetsimplevegan.com/vegan-cheesecake-brownies/

Caison, B. (2021, January 29). *Upgrade homemade vegetable stock to make the best-ever vegan ramen.* Delish. https://www.delish.com/cooking/recipe-ideas/a35131769/vegan-ramen/

Caldwell, N. (n.d.). *10 Benefits of a plant-based diet.* Thistle. https://www.thistle.co/learn/thistle-thoughts/10-benefits-of-a-plant-based-diet

Cookie and Kate. (2017, June 19). *Pink drink.* https://cookieandkate.com/pink-drink-recipe/

Davison, C. (2022, January 19). *Beginner's guide to a plant-based diet.* Forks over Knives. https://www.forksoverknives.com/how-tos/plant-based-primer-beginners-guide-starting-plant-based-diet/

Donahue, A. (2020, March 11). *These are the essentials you need to stock your plant-based pantry.* MamaSezz. https://www.mamasezz.com/blogs/news/how-to-stock-your-plant-based-pantry

Donahue, A. (2021, August 26). *What is a plant-*

based diet? What to eat and avoid. MamaSezz. https://www.mamasezz.com/blogs/news/what-are-plant-based-foods

Donofrio, J., & Donofrio, J. (2016a, June 6). *Summer strawberry crumble*. Love and Lemons. https://www.loveandlemons.com/strawberry-crumble/

Donofrio, J., & Donofrio, J. (2016b, November 12). *Pumpkin pudding recipe*. Love and Lemons. https://www.loveandlemons.com/pumpkin-pudding/

Donofrio, J., & Donofrio, J. (2017a, March 28). *Best Buddha bowl*. Love and Lemons. https://www.loveandlemons.com/buddha-bowl-recipe/

Donofrio, J., & Donofrio, J. (2017b, May 4). *Vegan pimento cheese dip*. Love and Lemons. https://www.loveandlemons.com/pimento-cheese/

Donofrio, J., & Donofrio, J. (2018, August 6). *Avocado summer rolls recipe*. Love and Lemons. https://www.loveandlemons.com/summer-rolls/

Donofrio, J., & Donofrio, J. (2019, August 5).

Baba ganoush. Love and Lemons. https://www.loveandlemons.com/baba-ganoush/

Donofrio, J., & Donofrio, J. (2020a, August 6). *Vegan ranch dressing*. Love and Lemons. https://www.loveandlemons.com/vegan-ranch-dressing/

Donofrio, J., & Donofrio, J. (2020b, December 8). *French onion dip*. Love and Lemons. https://www.loveandlemons.com/french-onion-dip-recipe/

Duclos, A. (2016, July 11). *"Nacho" vegan baked potato recipe*. Forks over Knives. https://www.forksoverknives.com/recipes/vegan-baked-stuffed/nacho-baked-potato/

Fisher, C. (2021, November 15). *Best-ever beefless stew*. Forks over Knives. https://www.forksoverknives.com/recipes/vegan-soups-stews/best-ever-beefless-stew/

Food Network Kitchen. (n.d.-a). *The best crispy tofu*. https://www.foodnetwork.com/recipes/food-network-kitchen/the-best-crispy-tofu-8317073

Food Network Kitchen. (n.d.-b). *Vegan "pulled pork" sliders*. Food Network. https://www.foodnetwork.com/recipes/food-network-kitchen/vegan-pulled-pork-sliders-3364735

Forks Over Knives. (2016, January 20). *Egyptian breakfast beans (Ful medames).* https://www.forksoverknives.com/recipes/ vegan-breakfast/egyptian-breakfast-beans-ful-medames/

Forks Over Knives. (2017, January 23). *Orange French   toast.* https://www.forksoverknives.com/recipes/ vegan-breakfast/orange-french-toast/

Fountaine, S. (2021, July 3). *Southwest black bean quinoa salad.* Feasting at Home. https://www.feastingathome.com/black-bean-quinoa-salad/

Fountaine, S. (2022, May 13). *Soba noodle salad.* Feasting at Home. https://www.feastingathome.com/sesame-soba-noodles-with-smoked-salmon-and-cucumber/

Frey, M. (2021, October 11). *What is a plant-based diet?* Verywell Fit. https://www.verywellfit.com/plant-based-diet-recipes-tips-guidelines-4174728

Goldman, H. (2018, August 6). *Strawberry-mango Hawaiian shave ice.* PureWow. https://www.purewow.com/recipes/strawb erry-mango-hawaiian-shave-ice

GoMacro. (n.d.). *How to start a plant-based diet.* https://www.gomacro.com/how-to-start-a-plant-based-diet/

Gorin, A. (2020, August 4). *Vegan chocolate dairy-free pudding*. Plant Based with Amy. https://plantbasedwithamy.com/the-healthiest-vegan-chocolate pudding/

Green Evi. (2018, September 28). *Vegan tomato flatbread*. http://greenevi.com/vegan-tomato-flatbread/

Gurney, B. (2022, March 18). *What is a plant-based diet? Facts and myths you should know*. Keck Medicine of USC. https://www.keckmedicine.org/blog/what-is-a-plant-based-diet/

Hama, J. (2021, February 19). *Vegan jalapeno poppers (Gluten free)*. Plant Based Folk. https://plantbasedfolk.com/vegan-jalapeno-poppers/

Hill, A. (2019, July 8). *23 Tips to ease meal prep*. Healthline. https://www.healthline.com/nutrition/meal-prep-tips#TOC_TITLE_HDR_1

Hingle, R. (2019, March 14). *Vegan Nashville hot cauliflower bites*. Vegan Richa. https://www.veganricha.com/vegan-nashville-hot-cauliflower-bites/

Huggins, M. (2017, June 29). *Roasted red pepper sandwich w/ vegan mozzarella*. Vegan Huggs.

https://veganhuggs.com/roasted-red-pepper-sandwich-vegan-mozzarella/

Johnson, L. (2020, June 20). *Orange peach mango spritzer*. Cooking with Curls. https://cookingwithcurls.com/2016/05/31/orange-peach-mango-spritzer/

Katia. (2019, October 8). *Beetroot hummus in 5 minutes!* The Clever Meal. https://theclevermeal.com/beetroot-hummus-in-5-minutes/

Kubala, J. (2018, June 12). *Whole-foods, plant-based diet: A detailed beginner's guide*. Healthline. https://www.healthline.com/nutrition/plant-based-diet-guide

Lakshminarayan, P. (2020, April 22). *Dairy-free dalgona coffee*. Cookilicious. https://cookilicious.com/dairy-free-dalgona-coffee/

Lienard, S. (2019). *What is a plant-based diet?* BBC Good Food. https://www.bbcgoodfood.com/howto/guide/what-plant-based-diet

Luna, M. (2020, May 19). *Cauliflower leek soup (vegan)*. Where You Get Your Protein. https://www.whereyougetyourprotein.com/cauliflower-leek-soup/

McManus, K. (2018, September 27). *What is a plant-based diet and why should you try it?*.

Harvard Health Blog. https://www.health.harvard.edu/blog/what-is-a-plant-based-diet-and-why-should-you-try-it-2018092614760

Merchant, J. (2019, March 6). *Slow roasted tomato hummus*. How Sweet Eats. https://www.howsweeteats.com/2019/03/slow-roasted-tomato-hummus/

Minimalist Baker. (2017, December 6). *Crispy gluten-free eggplant parmesan*. Minimalist Baker. https://minimalistbaker.com/crispy-gluten-free-eggplant-parmesan/

Minimalist Baker. (2018, May 22). *Creamy golden milk smoothie*. https://minimalistbaker.com/creamy-golden-milk-smoothie/

Minimalist Baker. (2020, October 3). *Vegan caesar salad with BBQ sweet potato croutons*. Minimalist Baker. https://minimalistbaker.com/vegan-caesar-salad-with-bbq-sweet-potato-croutons/

Natalie. (2018, June 18). *Blueberry latte breakfast smoothie jars*. Feasting on Fruit. https://feastingonfruit.com/blueberry-latte-breakfast-smoothie-jars/

New World. (n.d.). *Salted caramel banana split*. https://www.newworld.co.nz/recipes/desse

rts/salted-caramel-banana-split

Nicole. (2018, January 3). *Dessert smoothie bowls (3 ways).* When Sweet Becomes Healthy. https://whensweetbecomeshealthy.com/dessert-smoothie-bowls-3-ways/

Overhiser, S. (2017, March 21). *"Bliss bites" healthy no-bake cookies.* A Couple Cooks. https://www.acouplecooks.com/bliss-bites-healthy-no-bake-cookies/

Overhiser, S. (2020a, August 10). *Acai smoothie.* A Couple Cooks. https://www.acouplecooks.com/acai-smoothie/

Overhiser, S. (2020b, October 24). *Go-to vegan pancakes.* A Couple Cooks. https://www.acouplecooks.com/vegan-pancakes/

Save The Food. (n.d.). *10 Easy tips for meal planning.* Retrieved July 3, 2022, from https://savethefood.com/articles/10-easy-tips-for-meal-planning

Sczebel, C. (2018, April 22). *Healthy almond pistachio frozen yogurt (Dairy free).* Nutrition in the Kitch. https://nutritioninthekitch.com/healthy-almond-pistachio-frozen-yogurt-no-ice-cream-machine-needed/

Smith, D. (2016, October 19). *Crustless broccoli*

sun-dried tomato quiche. Plant Based Cooking. https://www.plantbasedcooking.com/recip e/crustless-tofu-quiche/

Sroufe, D. (2015a, April 13). *Cauliflower breakfast scramble*. Forks over Knives. https://www.forksoverknives.com/recipes/ vegan-breakfast/cauliflower-breakfast-scramble/

Sroufe, D. (2015b, September 5). *Healthy oatmeal recipe with fruits and nuts*. Forks over Knives. https://www.forksoverknives.com/recipes/ vegan-breakfast/fruit-and-nut-healthy-oatmeal/

Szeliga, E. (2021, September 3). *Georgian eggplant rolls with walnuts*. Happy Kitchen. https://happykitchen.rocks/georgian-eggplant-rolls-with-walnuts/

The Edgy Veg. (2020, July 25). *Maple garlic sauce*. https://www.theedgyveg.com/2020/07/24 /maple-garlic-sauce/

The Edgy Veg. (2021, June 5). *Vegan hollandaise sauce recipe*. https://www.theedgyveg.com/2021/06/05/ vegan-hollandaise-sauce/

Unlock Food. (2020, November 24). *10 Tips for planning meals on a budget*.

https://www.unlockfood.ca/en/Articles/Budget/10-Tips-for-Planning-Meals-on-a-Budget.aspx

VanderMolen, F. (2022, April 6). *Vegan breakfast burritos (Freezer-friendly!)*. The Conscientious Eater. https://theconscientiouseater.com/vegan-breakfast-burritos/

Vora, N. (2021a, May 25). *Herbed vegan potato salad*. Rainbow Plant Life. https://rainbowplantlife.com/herbed-vegan-potato-salad/

Vora, N. (2021b, June 4). *No-bake cookie dough bars (Vegan & gluten-free)*. Rainbow Plant Life. https://rainbowplantlife.com/no-bake-cookie-dough-bars/

Vora, N. (2022a, January 13). *Roasted butternut squash kale salad*. Rainbow Plant Life. https://rainbowplantlife.com/roasted-butternut-squash-and-cabbage-salad/

Vora, N. (2022b, February 28). *Fudgy vegan chocolate truffles*. Rainbow Plant Life. https://rainbowplantlife.com/vegan-chocolate-truffles/

Wendel, D. T. (2022, February 4). *Light Thai peanut dressing*. Forks over Knives. https://www.forksoverknives.com/recipes/vegan-sauces-condiments/light-thai-peanut-dressing/

Whitmore, C. (2015, May 20). *Summer drink recipe: Blackberry coolers*. Pizzazzerie. https://pizzazzerie.com/recipes/summer-drink-recipe-blackberry-coolers/

Wright, L. (2017, October 11). *Butternut minestrone with sage, chickpeas & chard*. The First Mess. https://thefirstmess.com/2017/10/11/vegan-butternut-minestrone-recipe/

Yzquierdo, H. (2014, September 24). *Easy vegan spinach artichoke dip*. My Plant-Based Family. https://myplantbasedfamily.com/2014/09/24/spinach-artichoke-dip/

Image References

APA Avice, L. (2021). *Creamy chickpea.* Unsplash. [Image]. https://unsplash.com/photos/yr-sW_x9aHk

Doan, T. (2018). *Top View Photo of Food Dessert.* Pexels. [Image]. https://www.pexels.com/photo/top-view-photo-of-food-dessert-1099680/

Drndarski, T. (2020). *Dalgona coffee with fresh coconut milk and white chocolate.* Unsplash. [Image]. https://unsplash.com/photos/TaCNAGSC9g4

Dubler, S. (2018). *Summer Crumble.* Unsplash. [Image]. https://unsplash.com/photos/sHCAlf-xA5U

Gravy, D. (2021). *Flatflay of flatbread pizza on a dark background.* Unsplash. [Image]. https://unsplash.com/photos/A4gYdu81kig

Heftiba, T. (2017). *French Toast.* Unsplash. [Image]. https://unsplash.com/photos/0XGWys_GaF0

Makafood. (2021). *Soup With Sliced Tomato and Green Leaf Vegetable in Black Cooking Pot.* Pexels. [Image]. https://www.pexels.com/photo/food-dinner-lunch-meal-8954298/

McCarty, D. (2020). *Pommes frites. Chips. Fried potatoes.* Unsplash. [Image]. https://unsplash.com/photos/kZBPmduhA PY

McCutcheon, S. (2018). *Tilt Shift Lens Photography of Five Assorted Vegetables.* Pexels. [Image]. https://www.pexels.com/photo/tilt-shift-lens-photography-of-five-assorted-vegetables-1196516/

McPhee, A. (2018). *Cilantro.* Unsplash. [Image]. https://unsplash.com/photos/yWG-ndhxvqY

Mirhashemian, A. (2020). *Fudgy Chocolate Truffles.* Unsplash. [Image]. https://unsplash.com/photos/V8Bc1BhXG vE

Olsson, E. (2018). *Photo of Vegetable Salad in Bowls.* Pexels. [Image]. https://www.pexels.com/photo/photo-of-vegetable-salad-in-bowls-1640770/

Olsson, E. (2018). *Plant-based meal prep.* Unsplash. [Image]. https://unsplash.com/photos/lMcRyBx4G5 o

Shaikh, N. (2021). *Oriental noodle soup with herbs and chopsticks.* Pexels. [Image]. https://www.pexels.com/photo/oriental-noodle-soup-with-herbs-and-chopsticks-7758254/

Shes, V. (2021). *[Introduction]*. Unsplash. [Image]. https://unsplash.com/photos/4MEL9XS-3JQ

Tankilevitch, P. (2020). *Glass Jars on Wooden Shelf*. Pexels. [Image]. https://www.pexels.com/photo/glass-jars-on-wooden-shelf-3735147/

Total Shape. (2019). *Scrabble Pieces On A Plate*. Pexels. [Image]. https://www.pexels.com/photo/scrabble-pieces-on-a-plate-2377045/

Tuksar, D. (2019). *Sweet Veggie Smoothie*. Unsplash. [Image]. https://unsplash.com/photos/hsTwPUzFegQ

Tweten, C. (2019). *[Zesty Caesar Salad]*. Unsplash. [Image]. https://unsplash.com/photos/FK-UKNip0pE

Veronika FitArt. (2021). *[Cauliflower and Leek Soup]*. Unsplash. [Image]. https://unsplash.com/photos/j6MRFmGDlqc

Printed in Great Britain
by Amazon

84676016R00139